PRAISE FOR

Dining AT THE WHITE HOUSE

"I found the book authentic, engaging, and enjoyable. Many of the chefs (and there have not been that many) who have worked in the White House Executive Residence kitchens have written cookbooks with references to their interactions with the First Families. John's is among the best!

Many have claimed to work for First Families and to have prepared both their personal meals and the official dinners and events of the presidency, but only a few actually own that claim. Some who worked in the military facilities like the Navy Mess in the West Wing or the Presidential Retreat at Camp David claim to be presidential chefs or cooks but that is different and distinct from the men and women who truly worked on a daily basis to provide the best American food to the president, his family and their guests."

— *Gary Walters, White House Chief Usher, 1986–2007*

"*Dining at the White House* is the personal tale of a budding young American chef, tutored in classic French cuisine, whose boundless creative energy and hard work propel him into our beloved White House — one of the world's most elegant and storied executive residences. John Moeller's experiences in serving three presidents reveal the great diversity of events and styles as the White House kitchen stretches itself to present the evolving new American fusion cuisine, which is based on the use of only the freshest, superior ingredients. The book's final treat is the selection of appealing and manageable recipes served to both American and international dignitaries — and now even we novices can try them!"

— *Catherine S. Fenton, Former Special Assistant to the President, and White House Social Secretary*

"You've no doubt seen the delectable meals served at the White House featured in a documentary or perhaps in movies. Our mouths have watered, but we will most likely never get to sample the offerings. Now, however, we have the next best thing: a book that delves into the mystical and mouthwatering world of White House meals, written by John Moeller, a chef who had the honor of cooking for three First Families and preparing amazing dishes for dignitaries from around the world.

The book is a treasure-trove of behind-the-scenes stories, not just of cooking but also of all things related to what it's like to live in the White House. This is a great source for enthusiasts of 'everything White House' as well as for fans of cooking. What sums it up best is a quote from Moeller, who explains that the staff was serving a 'real family in a real home,' but also that 'it was like working in a country club with a busy banquet facility.'

A delectable treat for those who want to learn what it's really like inside the White House, as well as for those who want a taste of some of the delicious meals served to presidents."

— *Feathered Quill Book Reviews*

"In *Dining at the White House*, John Moeller strikes a wonderful balance. From the very first nervous moment during a luncheon when he is bidden in to meet his first First Lady, Barbara Bush, through the Clintons' millennium celebrations, to his last day when his family joins him in a meeting with President George W. Bush at "the office," Moeller gives us the factual history yet offers it in a personal narrative that is refreshingly simple and direct. The book is well balanced between text and descriptions and the images of mouthwatering meals and recipes served at the White House that punctuate it."

— *Carl Sferrazza Anthony, author of* First Ladies *(2 vols.) and*
America's First Families, *and Historian of the National First Ladies Library*

"Chef Moeller has very accurately captured the essence of working in the White House. He vividly creates a true sense of the history of the time through his personal anecdotes while also sharing the cuisine and dining experiences from the inside perspective of the kitchen. I will forever look back fondly at the time I was privileged to share my kitchen with him."

— *Pierre Chambrin, White House Executive Chef, 1992–1994*

"A must-read book for any serious foodie, full of adventure and an inside look into the White House from a chef's viewpoint."

— *Gerry Quinn, Executive Chef & owner, Quinn's South Beach*

Dining
AT THE
WHITE HOUSE

FROM THE PRESIDENT'S TABLE TO YOURS

JOHN MOELLER
with MIKE LOVELL

AMERICAN LIFESTYLE PUBLISHING
LANCASTER, P.A.

DINING AT THE WHITE HOUSE:
From the President's Table to Yours

Editor@LifeReloaded.com

AMERICAN LIFESTYLE PUBLISHING
an imprint of LifeReloaded Specialty Publishing LLC, Lancaster, PA
www.LifeReloaded.com

Cover Design: Steve Cooley, Kemp Goldberg Partners
Book Design: Michael Brechner, Cypress House
Editor: Mike Lovell, LifeReloaded Specialty Publishing

Permissions: Photographs of Lenox Presidential china used with kind permission of Lenox Corporation • Photographs from the George Bush Presidential Library and Museum provided by the George Bush Presidential Library and Museum • Photographs from the William J. Clinton Presidential Library provided by the William J. Clinton Presidential Library • Photographs from the George W. Bush Presidential Library and Museum provided by the George W. Bush Presidential Library and Museum • Photographs of desserts at the White House used with kind permission of Chef Roland Mesnier • Photograph of Mrs. Julia Child in the White House kitchen used with kind permission of Rachel Walker • Back cover photograph of John Moeller used with kind permission of Mark Schafer.

ISBN: 978-1-60800-013-5-(Hardcover)

ISBN: 978-1-60800-022-7-(eBook)

PUBLISHER'S CATALOGING-IN-PUBLICATION DATA

Moeller, John.
    Dining at the White House : from the President's table to yours / John Moeller with Mike Lovell. -- 1st ed. -- Lancaster, PA : American Lifestyle Publishing, c2013.
        p. ; cm.
    ISBN: 978-1-60800-013-5
    Includes index.
    1. White House (Washington, D.C.)--History. 2. Cookery, American. 3. Dinners and dining--United States--History. 4. Washington (D.C.)--Social life and customs. I. Lovell, Mike. II. Title. III. From the President's table to yours.
    TX731 .M64 2013   2013938999
    642/.4--dc23   0913

DESIGNED, PUBLISHED AND PRINTED IN THE UNITED STATES OF AMERICA

2 4 6 8 9 7 5 3 1
First Edition

DEDICATION

I dedicate this book to my family, and thank them for their support

To my brother Mike, who passed away in 2010,

and who prompted me to move back home and get this book started

And to all the great chefs that I have learned from,

and to that grand tradition of chefs who continue to

pass on their great recipes and techniques to the next generation.

CONTENTS

The Road to the White House

President George H. W. Bush
and Mrs. Barbara Pierce Bush
(1992–1993)

Luncheon Menu for the President of the
Russian Federation: November 2001

President William J. Clinton and
Mrs. Hillary Rodham Clinton
(1993–2001)

MENU FOR A HOLIDAY DINNER AT THE WHITE HOUSE ON DECEMBER 3, 2004

PRESIDENT GEORGE W. BUSH AND MRS. LAURA WELCH BUSH (2001–2005)

FAREWELL TO THE WHITE HOUSE

Dining
AT THE
WHITE HOUSE

INTRODUCTION

Have you ever wondered what it would be like to dine at the White House? For thirteen years I was privileged to serve as a chef to three First Families. I was part of a team responsible for creating the dining experience at the White House and providing a wide variety of meals, from formal state dinners to outdoor picnics for hundreds to small intimate dinners for the President and First Lady and their guests.

The events that I describe in this book are as I experienced them in my role as a chef. Conversations have been recalled from memory; while not necessarily strictly verbatim, they represent the actual sense of the conversations to the best of my recollection.

The photographs and materials in the book are mostly from my own collection of official White House photos and memorabilia. There are also a few photos by courtesy of the presidential libraries and other sources included to illustrate events and provide the reader with a more complete experience. Throughout the book I have included about a dozen photos of selected dishes that were especially recreated for this book. These show exactly how meals were plated and presented at the White House.

From my early years I always had a passion for cooking. Eventually, it inspired me to make a journey to France, driven by the feeling that "there was something more out there." In the first part of the book I describe my own culinary journey as a chef, and how this spontaneous visit to France turned into a two-year adventure during which I lived with the local people, worked in the vineyards during the grape harvest, and had the opportunity to gain a deep understanding of the French approach to cooking and its strong connection to regional styles and fresh local ingredients.

Little did I think that these experiences abroad would turn out to be the critical factors that would give me the opportunity for a career at the White House a few years later.

There are three main sections devoted to each of the three First Families that I served during my thirteen years at the White House. I joined service there in September 1992, in the last few months of the presidency of George

H. W. Bush and First Lady Barbara Bush. In addition to describing what it was like serving the Bushes, this section includes a description of my early experience of working there and how food service at the White House works. This was also the time of the first of the many visits that I made to Camp David over the following thirteen years.

One of the highlights of the annual calendar is Christmas at the White House, and it was a great surprise to me to find that Christmas preparations had started early in the year and were well underway by the time I arrived in September.

In the section devoted to the presidency of William Jefferson Clinton and First Lady Hillary Rodham Clinton, I describe Mrs. Clinton's vision of transforming the menu at the White House to reflect a modern American cuisine, and how in 1994 she brought in Walter Scheib as the new executive chef. We created many innovative menus as we explored this new direction. It was particularly exciting for me, since the concepts of the new American cuisine incorporated many of the foundations of French cuisine, with its focus on regional cooking and using fresh, locally grown seasonal produce.

This section includes a small selection of the wide variety of our menus from the Clinton era to illustrate some of the creative new dishes that we were developing at that time.

The White House is also the peoples' house, and the sampling of menus and event cards included here illustrate the wide range of events such as Medal of Honor Awards, tributes to celebrate women leaders, etc., that are continually hosted at the White House year-round.

The Clinton era was also noted for its style of entertaining, and I've included a description of how we catered for some of the major events such as state dinners and large outdoor affairs where we served sit-down dinners to as many as 950 people at a time.

Working at the White House, we had an eyewitness view of history as it happened. Providing service to world leaders and dignitaries presents a unique set of challenges, whether in the White House itself, at Camp David, or at outside locations. The President and First Lady rely on the experience of their staff to maintain high levels of security and ensure that first-class standards are upheld. In this section I've included a description of several of the major events for which we traveled to locations outside of Washington, D.C.

The presidency of George W. Bush and First Lady Laura Bush started out with a great emphasis on kids and American family life, with activities such as Tee Ball on the South Lawn. However, that focus was later tragically overshadowed by the terrorist attacks of 9/11.

All Americans have their own memories of that terrible day. Although words can never suffice, I've tried to convey the surreal experience of being evacuated from the White House, walking through the streets of Washington, and eventually finding my way back home. The aftermath was a period of confusion and adjustment for everyone, and it was a unique set of experiences for those of us actually working at the White House. While there was an effort to return things to normal, it was a "new normal"—after 9/11 things were never the same again.

Walter Scheib's departure from his position as executive chef at the White House in 2005 set in motion a series of events that initially had me acting as White House Chef for a few months, during which Cristeta Comerford and I shared the workload. After Cris was appointed to succeed Walter as executive chef, I realized that it was time to look to my own future, and in November 2005 I resigned to pursue other interests.

In the recipe section I've included a selection of some thirty dishes and their component recipes from menus that I created and served at the White House. This is a self-contained section for the benefit of readers who may wish to jump directly to it. My aim here is to enable readers to bring the experience of dining at the White House to their own tables. With this in mind, the recipes have all been scaled to quantities and timing to serve six people, and some of the instructions have been simplified for the average home chef, who might not have the resources of a professional kitchen available.

Between the main parts of the book, I've included photo vignettes that show the recreation of two meals as they would have been presented at the White House. One is a luncheon in honor of President Putin's visit to the United States in 2001, and the other shows a holiday dinner served at the White house in 2004.

The pastry chef is a separate department in the White House, and has its own separate kitchens. Roland Mesnier was the executive pastry chef for twenty-five years until he left in 2004. Roland is the creative genius who developed the style of desserts for which the White House is justly famous.

Readers who are interested in dessert cooking will find wonderful recipes in Roland's own books.

The White House is a major center of power and influence throughout the world, and every day we were responsible for achieving the standards of quality and presentation that the President and First Lady were proud to offer to their visitors, whether world leaders, honored guests, or family members.

During my thirteen years at the White House I was privileged to serve three First Families. They always treated us well and with great consideration—they made us feel like family ourselves!

Working there, I was part of an inner circle that saw the president's family on a very personal level. We had to be mindful of that all the time and never compromise their privacy. No one I knew while working at the White House would ever break that trust— that would be like betraying our own family.

PROLOGUE

We'd just begun to serve the main course for the 1999 Sara Lee Front-runner Awards luncheon.

What's taking the butler so long to get that first plate out?

When the butler did get back to the kitchen, he told us that the White House Social Secretary, Capricia Marshall, had caught him just before he entered the dining room. Seeing our presentation, she exclaimed, "What a great-looking plate!" and she grabbed the photographer and swept him and the butler into the Red Room for a quick photo shoot.

Chicken with Pesto, Potato and Goat Cheese Purée, Broccoli, Carrots, and Shiitake Mushrooms, Chardonnay Reduction; Parsley Wafer.

The social secretary was especially delighted because world-renowned chef Julia Child was among the guests that day. Our smooth-running routine hesitated momentarily as news of the famous visitor rippled through the kitchen, but we were in full event mode, and though I felt a bit uneasy, I had no time to worry about what Mrs. Child might think of our efforts. I was concentrating on my top priorities: to make sure everyone executed his or her job properly, and to get each dish out there exactly as I wanted it.

When I was assigned responsibility for planning and preparing this luncheon, I had no reason to think it would stand out from among other White House events that month. As usual, the social secretary told us in general what the First Lady wanted, and I'd heard that most of the guests would be women. Beyond that, I had no idea who was on the guest list, so I followed the usual procedure and wrote up the menu for review by the social secretary and the First Lady.

LUNCHEON

On the occasion of the
1999 Sara Lee Frontrunner Awards

Fennel Scented
Kuri Squash and Leek Soup

Chicken with Pesto
Potato and Goat Cheese Purée
Broccoli, Carrots and Shiitake Mushrooms
Chardonnay Reduction   *Parsley Wafer*

Autumn Greens with Artichoke
Cucumber and Pear Tomato
Balsamic Mustard Dressing

"Frontrunner's Sweet Harvest"
Pumpkin Mousse   *Crystallized Ginger*
Poached Apple   *Blackberry Sauce*

TALLEY *Chardonnay "Estate" 1997*

The White House
Thursday, October 21, 1999

Luncheon menu for the 1999 Sara Lee Frontrunner Awards. The Frontrunner award is given to women whose accomplishments have shaped our past and given inspiration for the future. First Lady Hillary Rodham Clinton presented Julia Child with this award at the luncheon. October 21, 1999.

Ninety percent of the time, they would approve our menus on the first pass. Sometimes they'd send one back with a suggestion or two, and once in a while they might even request a tasting, but there was nothing unusual about this menu. Everything came together perfectly. As we finished, the White House Executive Chef, Walter Scheib, turned to me and said, "Everyone up there seems very happy—and Mrs. Child wants to come down and visit our kitchen."

The legendary chef entered the kitchen a few moments later, all smiles, and pronounced her assessment of our work: "Oh, everything was great!" Approval from such a highly respected professional can make all that hard work feel worth the extra effort. Luckily, one of our staff members happened to have a camera with her, so we were able to capture our proud moment in a photo of Julia Child with Walter and me standing on either side.

Julia Child meets with (from left) Paula Patton-Moutsos, Francis O'Day, Cristeta Comerford, Walter Scheib, John Moeller, David Leursen, and Clarence Lipford in the White House kitchen, October 21, 1999.
Courtesy Rachel Walker.

It's probably a good thing I didn't know Mrs. Child was scheduled as a guest. Who knows—I might have had second thoughts about the menu. Perhaps I'd have made changes that she wouldn't have found so pleasing. Not knowing can be an advantage; you just do your best without overthinking the whole process. To top it all off, I was in the ushers' office a week later when one of the ushers on duty asked, "You worked that luncheon that Julia Child attended, right?"

"Yeah," I replied, "that was my menu."

He handed me a letter and said, "This just came from Julia Child."

103 IRVING STREET
CAMBRIDGE, MASSACHUSETTS 02138
617·876·1072

October 26, 1999

Hillary Rodham Clinton
The White House
Washington, DC

Dear Mrs. Clinton:

How very kind of you to host a luncheon for all of us the other day in your beautiful White House. I have been there several times, starting with the LBJ administration, where everything was beautifully handled.

During subsequent visits, I was not as impressed. But, when I returned for the Sara Lee Frontrunner awards luncheon, I was delighted to find the White House sparkling, and the service beautiful and attentive, and the food delicious. It was a very heartwarming experience.

Thank you so much. With all good wishes

Julia Child

Letter from Julia Child to First Lady Hillary Rodham Clinton expressing her appreciation for the luncheon to mark the Sara Lee Frontrunner awards.

THE WHITE HOUSE

November 9, 1999

Ms. Julia Child
103 Irving Street
Cambridge, Massachusetts 02138

Dear Julia:

Thank you for your very thoughtful letter about our Sara Lee Frontrunner luncheon. I will be sure to share it with Chef Scheib and our residence staff. I know they will be thrilled to receive your accolades. It was wonderful seeing you again.

With warm regards, I remain

Sincerely yours,

Hillary Rodham Clinton

cc: Capricia Marshall, Social Secretary
       Gary Walters, Chief Usher
       Walter Scheib, White House Chef

Letter of acknowledgment from
First Lady Hillary Rodham Clinton to Julia Child.

Mrs. Child's letter described how much she had enjoyed her luncheon at the White House. From the moment of her arrival, she was impressed with how clean and fresh everything appeared. The decorations looked great, and the service and food were spectacular. This experience had completely revised her opinions about the White House and its cuisine. "Wow!" I said. "Can I make a photocopy of this?"

"Absolutely."

Then, as I was copying the letter, he held out another piece of paper and said, "There's this one, too."

In his hand was Mrs. Clinton's response to Mrs. Child, thanking her for her kind words about the luncheon. I copied that one, too, of course, as another memento of that day—a very good day.

THE ROAD
to the
WHITE HOUSE

A Taste for the Business

How does a kid from the heart of Pennsylvania Dutch country end up cooking for international heads of state at the White House?

I've always had a great passion for cooking. I remember early on, in high school, thinking about taking culinary classes. My parents had bought me an intriguing book called *The Great Chefs of France*, and I believe cheffing is how it was worded. I was wowed by descriptions of the painstaking effort chefs would go through and how they dedicated their lives to producing quality meals. As my own career as a chef developed, I would often think back to that book and I would wonder, *What's the next level? How do I get to that point?*

I started my own career at the Willow Street Vo-Tech (now the Lancaster County Career and Technology Center) in Willow Street, Pennsylvania, and then went on to the Culinary School at Johnson & Wales University in Providence, Rhode Island.

On graduation day at Johnson & Wales in 1981, one of my teachers offered us graduates an invitation to join in a trip to Europe. It would start in England, then on to Scotland, Ireland, and Wales, and finally to France. In all, we would spend two weeks traveling.

I'd never been to Europe, so everything was new, and exploring the culinary aspect of it was very intriguing. We ate at a variety of restaurants, and we experienced many new and different things there. Without a doubt, that heightened my interest and laid the groundwork for my work experience in France that was to come later.

Before we headed up north to Scotland, we stayed in London for a couple of days. My first meal in England was at a small local restaurant, and I remember having a mushroom soup. I thought, *Oh, my God! I've never tasted anything like this before!* And I talked to someone at the restaurant, trying to get a little insight. "What was in that? It was so good! Wow, there's something different here. How can I learn that?" And, tasting some dishes that were different from what I'd ever had back in the States was part of what compelled me, a couple of years later, to say, "I want to go back there and study how they do it."

As I later learned, it was a combination of cooking and ingredients. Maybe it was just a white mushroom, but it was likely grown in a cave and that gave it a whole different character. In Paris, what they call *les champignons de Paris* (mushrooms of Paris) were also simple white mushrooms, but they're grown in these old, unused railway tunnels beneath the city. Of course, the conditions are perfect for growing mushrooms, and the flavor that came out of this raw environment of the tunnels was totally amazing.

That concept of how superior ingredients can make such a tremendous difference in the result was a huge influence for me. It has carried over into everything I have done throughout my career, and it's what still drives me today. I'm very picky with my ingredients, so I go out and select everything I get. I personally choose everything I cook with.

When we got to France, we students went out for lunch on our own on one occasion, without an organized tour. There were four or five of us, and we just found a restaurant. My French was limited. As I read over the menu, I knew the culinary terms, but I didn't know much else. I saw *le pied de veau*, and thought, *Hmm, a veal dish for lunch. That sounds pretty good.* Of course when the dish came out, it was the feet of the veal. And when I looked at this calf's foot on my plate, I thought, *What the hell am I supposed to do with this?* That veal dish didn't exactly thrill me, but it did kindle an interest: *Wow, they do really different things over here!* And, that was another of those things that lured me back to France two years later.

In a culinary sense, the rest of the graduation trip was decent but not extraordinary. It was just that mushroom soup that made such a lasting impression. It sparked a kind of "Holy Grail" in my head, something I wanted to be able to recreate, no matter what it took. Unfortunately, I never was able to get back to that restaurant—I can't even remember where it was—but I got the idea of a different way to make mushroom soup, and I was a happy person.

After we returned from our trip, I worked at a couple of little restaurants and hotels in Rhode Island, but there was always that nagging feeling—something inside me kept urging me to reach for that next level. I felt there had to be something more out there than what I was doing.

It seemed as if something was calling to me, saying, "Yes, if you have the opportunity, go back there."

By 1983, I was beginning to wonder if it was time to move away from Providence and explore new opportunities. Fueling that restlessness was my good friend and classmate Gerry Quinn, whom I'd known since we attended Lancaster County Career and Technology Center together. After we graduated from Johnson & Wales, he had decided to pursue his culinary career in Europe. The firstborn of Irish emigrants, Gerry was able to return to his parents' home and reclaim Irish citizenship. Once he had an Irish passport, he could easily move about the European Union and find work. He began in an Irish restaurant, and soon had an opportunity to work at its sister restaurant in Paris.

Gerry had been urging me for a good while to come to Europe and check out the culinary scene. He kept writing to invite me for a visit or to try working over there. He persisted, and I began toying with the idea. I even started saving up my nickels and dimes and moonlighting to earn extra money, and in six months I had saved enough for a ticket.

OFF TO FRANCE

Finally, in 1984, when Gerry wrote and said, "John, you've gotta come over and give this a try." I decided, *Yes. I'm going back.* I wanted to see that next level—the things I'd read about in books, the things I'd experienced a little on that first trip to France. I wanted to try to develop something out of that. Little did I know that it was the perfect time to do so.

And, my previous two-week culinary tour of Britain and France helped me feel adventurous enough to head out on my own with just my backpack, a one-way ticket, and a guide to youth hostels.

Looking back, it wouldn't have worked if I had made an extended European trip right out of culinary school; I wasn't prepared enough. But after working for a while, and taking the trip over there when I was twenty-two, I was more mature and knew a lot more about cooking. I wouldn't have had enough experience to do that the first time around. In fact, the teacher who took us over there in 1981 had said, "If anyone wants to stay here in France and get some more experience, we could change your ticket. You could go to almost any restaurant here and they'd take you on for a little while. If you want to spend the rest of the summer here, then do it."

Just one person did, and she was back in less than a week. I'm emphasizing the point that if I had stayed, it probably wouldn't have been long before I'd have come back. I wasn't ready to turn a trip like that into a work experience.

At twenty-two, however, I was ready for it: I'd had some education, and could go into a kitchen with a fuller understanding and not be completely green. Most importantly, I had learned the basic disciplines that go with working as a chef in a professional kitchen. If you can show chefs that you know something already, they'll take the time to show you more. All the chefs I worked with were impressed at the fact that I wanted to learn, and they also recognized that I had some learning behind me, so they were willing to add to it.

I met up with Gerry once I arrived in Paris, but found living in the city a bit too expensive. After a week, I took a train toward Nice in the South of France, and decided to stop along the way to explore the countryside. I told Gerry, "I want to see what's going on down there, and I'll be back who knows when."

I got off the train at Dijon, about halfway to Nice, and headed to the local tourism office, where I followed my usual travel routine: find shelter for the night, and then figure out my food for the evening. By the time I located the tourism office and collected some brochures to help me find a campground, it was four in the afternoon. My French was next to useless, and I needed a place to sit and read the brochures. Literature in hand, I went outside and sat down to have a cigarette. A young man approached me and said something in French. I just looked at him and asked, "Do you speak English?"

"Yes," he replied. "Do you have an extra cigarette?"

I shared a smoke with him, and we chatted for a few moments. I found out that he lived nearby, so I held up a brochure and asked if he knew where the campground was. He nodded. "How do you plan to get there? It's at least a forty-five-minute walk. Are you traveling by yourself?"

"Yes, I'm alone. I just got off the train fifteen minutes ago."

"Then why don't you come along with me? I'm meeting some friends at a café downtown, and when my girlfriend gets off work, we're going to eat. You're welcome to join us, if you like."

When we arrived around seven o'clock, the little back-street restaurant in the middle of Dijon was empty. The regular dinner crowd wouldn't arrive till later. We ate couscous and did our best to communicate in an awkward mix of English and French. After a while, another customer arrived and took a table directly across the aisle. I did a double take when I noticed his T-shirt, which was printed with a picture of a horse and buggy. Underneath was the slogan PARADISE IS FOR LOVERS — PARADISE, PENNSYLVANIA. I asked him if he spoke English. When he said yes, I asked, "I'm curious: have you ever visited that place on your T-shirt?"

"Oh, yes!" he replied. "My wife has friends in Harrisburg. We were there a year ago. We traveled through Lancaster and stopped in Paradise—do you know this place?"

"Yeah! That's where I'm from—I grew up there!"

As we talked, he became part of our table's conversation, and once we'd all finished our meal, our new acquaintance—Jean-Marie—asked, "What are you guys doing tonight?"

We had no plans, so he invited us to his house for a drink. We walked two or three blocks to his place and continued our conversation over glasses of red wine. When my companions spoke French, I could barely follow along, but after an hour or so, Jean-Marie turned to me and asked in English if I had plans for the weekend. I explained that I was just touring the country and had no plans at all.

"Tomorrow evening, a friend and I are driving down to the Jura Valley, on the Swiss border, to meet my wife and children. The family has an old chalet in the hills there, and I'd like to invite you to join us for the weekend."

Of course I agreed, and we arranged to meet the next day. On Saturday we drove down to the village of St. Laurent, not far from Lausanne, Switzerland, where I met Jean-Marie's wife, Catherine, who was an English teacher, and her parents, who were teachers, also.

Other friends joined us, and we spent a joyous weekend in the French country-side savoring great food, drinking great wine, and visiting with great company. Late Sunday evening, the conversation turned to me. Everyone wanted to know what I was doing in France.

I explained that I was a chef by trade, and had worked for a few years in America. I had come to France at the urging of my friend in Paris, and was now checking out opportunities to work in French restaurants. They listened to my story, and then resumed their French conversation. After a few minutes, they turned back to me and Jean-Marie said, "Well, here's what we can offer you: we have an extra bedroom back in Dijon, and you're welcome to stay there as long as you'd like."

He told me that in August the local university would be offering special classes to help foreigners learn to speak French—and he volunteered to use his connections at the university to get me into the upcoming program.

"The first thing we need to do is to get you to learn French," he said. "We don't want you to feel obligated, but the offer's there if you want it."

Knowing that fluency in French would help me to find work, I accepted, and just like that, this backpacking tourist became a language student at the University of Dijon, with a place to live and a whole new routine. For the next month I'd go to school every day, and on weekends Jean-Marie would either take me back to see the family at Jura Valley or to visit one of the little villages just south of Dijon.

MAKING A FRENCH CONNECTION

With a smile and a gesture, Jean-Marie would say, "Let's go find something to eat," and off we'd go, driving into these little villages where he grew up. Here were his roots—and his old friends, who were all very interested in meeting his new American friend. That meant I found myself invited to nearly everyone's home. I learned a lot about local food and drink as we went from house to house tasting great dishes prepared by wonderful, down-to-earth people. Until I went to this region, I had never tasted Merguez, the red spicy sausage flavored with North African spices. These were thin sausages (like breakfast links in the States) that were made locally using lamb or mutton and typically served with couscous. And everyone had his own variation on how to make a salad; it was pretty much a point of honor to recognize the distinct characteristics of each household and how they prepared their salad dressing. (The basic ingredients are mustard, shallots, and vinaigrette. To this day, I still use the basic recipe of the region for my own salad, and it's included later in this book.)

Jean-Marie's friends enjoyed showing me how they made their favorite cocktails, especially the kir, for which Dijon is famed, and which is named after Félix Kir, formerly a longtime mayor of Dijon. This cocktail is made from a measure of *crème de cassis*—a specialty of the Burgundy region—topped with *aligoté* (a regional white wine). Kir was very popular in France long before it showed up in America, and it seemed everyone had his own way of making the cassis—the sweet blackcurrant liqueur—and each one would insist, "Here, try this," "Taste that," "Eat some of this," or "Drink a little more."

In September, when the family returned from holiday, we started a new routine. I had completed the summer language classes, and my friends encouraged me to stay on to attend the university full time. (I ended up studying French there for two full semesters.) Full-time classes wouldn't start until October, but the family went back to work and school right away. Like a typical French family, they all came home every day at noon for a ninety-minute lunch break. Since I had time on my hands, I took it upon myself to prepare lunch and have it ready for them when they arrived, thus becoming the "private chef on duty." Jean-Marie's wife, Catherine, was particularly thrilled at this arrangement, since it had always been her duty to race home from teaching school, turn on the stove, and fix lunch. Their custom was always to have a big, hot lunch, then make a lighter supper, often from leftovers, perhaps with a soup or a salad.

For lunch, I would serve meals such as vegetable potage — a potato and leek soup — medallions of pork, or a whole roasted chicken. A favorite of the family was a skillet platter made up of small steaks seared and mixed with vegetables.

A couple of blocks from the house was a small neighborhood market that operated most days of the week. Catherine would leave a few francs on the table when she headed out in the morning and say, "Buy whatever you like." It was a great experience for me to go down to this sidewalk market and discover the fresh produce of the region and practice my French haggling with the vendors.

Les Vendanges in Dijon

For two weeks right before the semester began, I had the opportunity to work *les vendanges* (the grape harvest) in the wine country south of Dijon. I was a grape picker in Meursault, south of Beaune, an area especially known for its white wines.

What an experience! For two weeks I lived with a large crew of harvesters in a grape farmer's barn. We were up every morning at 6:45, and gathered quickly for a *petit dejeuner* of croissants or *pain au chocolat* with *café au lait* or espresso. The women who prepared the food would also hand us a piece of baguette from which we made sandwiches for later in the morning. We had to be in the fields by seven o'clock, but we'd take our first break around 8:30. Sandwiches and wine starting at 8:30 in the morning — what a life! Then it was back to cutting grapes till noon. Lunch was a big meal, and we didn't return to the fields till 1:30. The workday lasted till 5:30 or 6:00 each evening, when we'd come in for supper.

Back at the barn, we showered, freshened up, and sat in the dining hall for a feast of country cooking complete with all the wine we could hold. An apparently endless supply of local wine flowed from bottles with no labels. After two fantastic weeks, I returned to Dijon and the family, ready to start my first semester of French at the university.

The entire experience of living on that farm with everyday working-class French people was great, too. It added to the joy of being there, instead of sitting in a hotel room or on a campus. Tons of kids went to the same school

I did — The University of Dijon — but all they did was go to class, come out, and speak English with their pals. I was living with a French family, and I was out in the streets seeing what was really going on. All of that just enhanced the whole experience.

At the end of September, Jean-Marie helped to arrange my first job in France.

One evening, while his family dined at a brand-new restaurant nearby, Jean-Marie mentioned to the owner that he knew "an American guy who wants to cook." The owner was interested enough to meet me, so I picked a night and stopped by the restaurant to meet him. He had worked in England, and his English was excellent. We got acquainted over drinks, and I learned that his restaurant had been open for a month. We talked about my background, what I wanted to do, and what I hoped to accomplish in the future. The dinner rush began to let up, and he looked around and said, "Just a minute — let me go back and talk to the chef."

He left me at the bar with my thoughts (and my single-malt Scotch) and disappeared into the kitchen. When he returned a few minutes later, he said, "All right, come on back with me. The chef wants to see your face."

I stood up to follow him, thinking, *All right, John, this is what you wanted, an entrée into a "real French kitchen."* We stepped inside, and before the doors stopped swinging behind me, my experience told me exactly what the chef was thinking: *We've only been open a few weeks. We're still getting organized, and I'm buried in work. I need real help, and this guy brings me an American chef?!*

At the cutting board, the chef, whose name was René, noisily chopped some vegetables, and then glanced up at me, a hint of contempt in his eyes. "American, huh?" His French accent was thick. He lowered his gaze. Chop, chop, chop, chop! He looked at me again. "American, huh? Hamburger? You hamburger, huh?" Chop, chop, chop, chop!

Feeling awkward, I replied, "Yeah, yeah… American hamburger… yeah, yeah." I tried to say something to him in French, but my language skills were still a bit shaky. It felt like one of the worst interviews ever, but to my surprise, he invited me to come back on Friday night.

"You're welcome to come and help us out. I can't pay you anything right now," he cautioned, "but I can feed you and maybe give you a couple drinks at the end of the night."

L'Estancot

Our relationship felt a little rocky at first, but we found ways to make it work. My French was rudimentary, but the chef patiently took time to help me with the language, and I continued to improve. I didn't have a regular schedule, and I wasn't getting paid, but as the place got busier we found a pretty good working rhythm. After a month or so, the owner approached me again. "John, the chef says he likes you, and asks if you'd like to start working regularly on Fridays and Saturdays. I can pay you a little — on the side."

L'Estancot was a typical French country bistro, tucked away in a back street behind Place Saint-Michel in Dijon — not at all touristy — the type of place where the locals would go to eat. Right away, I found myself cooking things that I had not seen before. *Cris de canard* (a piece of duck with the leg and thigh combined; *l'onglet frites* (hanger steak and fries; hanger steak comes from up underneath the rib and is not commonly available in the States); *Poulet de Bresse*, a breed of chicken that originated in eastern France between the Rhone River and the French Alps, and has a unique and exquisite flavor; and our customers liked Charolais beef, a light-skinned breed that originated in the Bourgogne Region of France.

Wine was very popular, of course, and the patrons would drink *vin ordinaire*, unlabeled local wines, served in pitchers or unlabeled bottles that had four stars molded into the glass around the neck.

My strategy was paying off: through patience and hard work, I now had a real part-time job. After a while it became full-time, and that busy little bistro became my genuine introduction to French cooking — and my first connection with the French culinary community. René was generous to a fault. On Mondays, when the restaurant was closed, he often invited me to go with him to the countryside. We would go fishing or visit with some of his friends. He showed me the area surrounding Dijon and introduced me to more foods and wines. In the end, René and I ended up working very well together, and he taught me the basics that I needed.

Though this was at the bistro level, it was still a step above many of the things I'd been working with back in the States. I wanted to absorb everything I could from René, and once we got the communication down and I was able to start conversing with him, I discovered the calendar at the end of the cooking line. At the top, the calendar had a picture of France, and the entire country was broken down into what is called *departments* (basically another word for states), and they showed pictures of different foods and where in the country they originated. Sometimes, if we were working with something I wasn't familiar with, René would bring me over to that picture of France and show me that this ingredient had come from this area and this from that area. Without that simple direction from him, it would've been just another mushroom on the cutting board, but he helped me understand the importance of where it came from; that is, if you go to that part of France, it would not have the same flavor and they might do things very differently there than where we were.

French cuisine is very regional. You travel 200 miles in France, and you're in a totally different area, preparing totally different dishes in entirely different ways, and even drinking different kinds of wine. The norm in Dijon isn't necessarily the norm elsewhere. You go down to Lyon and find that what they're doing in bistros there won't be the same as what goes on in Dijon. The people who lived there said they could never do what I did, just leave their home province and travel around. The people were as regional as the cuisine. René lived his whole life in Dijon. He told me, "I hardly ever went anywhere." In fact, after I had moved on and we had stopped working together, I went back for a visit, and he said to me, "John, you won't believe what I'm going to do."

"What's that?" I said.

He replied, "The owner of a restaurant where I used to be a chef now has a place in Costa Rica. He wants me to come down there and work for him. A year or two ago, I would've said, no way! I never would've done it, but because I met you, and saw what you went through to learn the French language and a whole new cuisine, I told myself, 'I can do that, too!'" With a smile, he looked at me and said, "I'm going!"

I had actually inspired this fifty-five-year-old chef to pack his bags and leave his homeland for the first time. Unfortunately, after I left that day, and René went to Costa Rica, we never had contact again, but I think of him often.

It made me feel great that my example helped him decide to take that trip. I hope he's well, and I'm sure he's loving the fishing down there.

René taught me how to cut up the different types of meat, such as *l'onglet*, that we didn't have over here in the States. We'd get produce in, and I would trim it down to make the portions for the restaurant menu. In a couple of months I was becoming proficient. Did I already have some knife skills? Did I know how to cut a piece of meat? Yes—but not the way René wanted it! That's part of cooking, too. Every restaurant and hotel and country club you go to, there's a different way of doing things. You're always going to walk away from anyplace having learned something different—something that you didn't see anywhere else. In France, I went from just cutting meat to really learning the subtleties of how to prepare it, and a lot of that came later, especially as I moved on to Chez Camille and then to Bernard Loiseau's Hotel de la Côte d'Or.

In France, all of our fish arrived whole, never as ready-to-cook fillets. They had the heads and gills and guts and fins—everything. We had to break them down altogether. One of the worst things I had to work with was quail. We'd get these whole little birds in, that still had the feathers, and I had to eviscerate them. Cleaning out these delicate quail wasn't easy, especially if you've got big hands like mine. Chicken was different, but I still had to be careful. If the knife slipped while I was removing the liver, I might pierce the gallbladder and spill bile on my cutting board. The bitter-tasting bile would ruin everything, and I'd have to start all over again. When I was done, I'd have one pile of all the innards and outers, as we called them, and then a plateful of the final product, the trimmed-out chicken parts ready for cooking. This was all part of the difference between cooking and cheffing: knowing how to prepare all these meats rather than just using commercially available products.

René also taught me how to break down a rabbit. One day, he and I were at his girlfriend's farm for a huge party that lasted from one in the afternoon till almost midnight. Before dinner started, there were some rabbits that needed to be prepared for cooking, so René grabbed a live rabbit and we went out to the barn. He killed and skinned the animal, and started to break it all down. That was the first time I'd ever seen the whole process, and I was intrigued by it. Whether you're looking at a rabbit, a lamb, a calf, or a cow, it's all the same layout. The carcasses may be bigger, but everything's in the same spot, and you can make all the same cuts.

I continued with René through the end of the school year, but having completed my language studies, I had started to feel that it was time to move on again. And, once again, the family provided me with the opportunity. Catherine had a friend who had been taking a hoteliers course at a local college where she had met the head chef at a fine-dining restaurant who was looking for an experienced chef, and she set up an interview for me.

The owner at L'Estancot was very disappointed that I was leaving—he had been setting up paperwork for me to be able to work there permanently. René was also sorry to see me go, but he said, *"J' comprends*—I fully understand."

CHEZ CAMILLE

Chez Camille was a quaint country inn located in Arnay-le-Duc in the Burgundy hill country west of Dijon. The ten-room inn featured a small dining room, and I learned traditional Burgundy-style cooking from M. Poinsot, one of the best chefs I've ever known.

At Chez Camille, a case of chickens came in one day. They still had the guts in them, still had the heads and feet on, they even had the pinfeathers on. The first thing I had to do was run the whole bird over a fire to burn off the pinfeathers. And at eight o'clock in the morning, the last thing you want to smell is burning feathers. It's not appetizing at all, and it's even worse if you've had a couple of drinks the night before. At first, it took me a long time to break down a case of chickens, because I had to dissect every one of them, remove all the guts and heads and feet and feathers, and then portion them out. Just preparing a chicken for cooking is completely different there than it is here in the States, where it usually comes prepped by the factory.

As a chef, once you've worked with a particular animal enough times, you understand the anatomy that's beneath all the meat, so when you go to stick your knife in, you know exactly where to put it. You think, *I'll run it alongside this bone, so I can get this portion. I'll punch it through here this way to get that one.* Every time I look at a carcass, I envision it with no meat on it, so I always know where to put the knife. That's how I view it, and that's how I teach it. The way I cut up a chicken is different from how it is usually done. When I demonstrate how to cut up a chicken, people say they've never seen it done that way. I don't smack it and bang it with a cleaver—I disarticulate the whole chicken and never crack a single bone. I teach the technique of how to pop a joint, run a knife through here and through there, and *boom*—you have the whole thing.

One of the lessons that I learned was to always keep the knife pointed toward the bone, so I cut, cut, cut, but I'm hitting the bone each time. I never have the knife pointed toward the meat. If, instead of going against the bone, the knife slices into a quality piece of meat, the meat is ruined, so whether it's rabbit or chicken or anything else, you always point the knife toward the bone. That way, it doesn't matter if you slip and hit the bone. But if you hit the money part of the meat and cut into it, you ruin what that piece of meat can offer, by bleeding out juices or by spoiling the presentation when you slice it after cooking.

Aside from damaging the meat and spoiling the presentation, one problem of using a cleaver is that it smashes bones and leaves the bone chips behind. Throughout the process, you use your sense of touch, which becomes refined over time. I run my hand across it, so I know it's just pure meat and also to make sure that the final product I'm going to serve has no shards of bone or cartilage or anything that someone could choke on or experience as unpleasant.

The step I had made from L'Estancot to the kitchen at Chez Camille was huge. For one thing, the chef had a lot of young apprentices, and he had one or two people who were a little more experienced, so he was there from morning till night almost every day of the season—he rarely took a day off.

He had a very calm personality, a quality uncommon among chefs. One evening, as we worked together behind the line, he took his *torchon* (dishcloth) and snapped it on the back of my calf. I looked at him and said, "Chef, what are you doing?" and he replied, "I have to start giving you some bruises, so when you go back to America you can say, 'Yeah, I worked at a French restaurant!'" That gentle joke exemplifies what an even-tempered guy he was. I never saw him get flustered.

Years later, in 2004, I took a trip to France with my family. As we went through Arnay-le-Duc, we came down an alleyway next to the back kitchen area. I was going to go in the front but I said, "I'll just try the door I used when I worked here." I knocked, and a guy came to the door. I said, "I'm looking for Chef Poinsot. Is he here?"

He replied, "Yeah—he's around back." I saw that the kitchen had been expanded, and was different from the kitchen I'd worked in. They had added an extra prep room in the back, so I went around a corner—and there was Poinsot!

He came over and looked at me and said, *"Comment ca va?"* (How are you?) I said, "I used to work for you back in 1984." He looked at me and said, "Yeah, I remember you—the American guy." The next thing out of his mouth was *"Tu est toujours en cuisine?"* (Are you still in the kitchen?) I said, *"Oui."* At that time I was still working in the White House, and I started to tell him about it. He was very, very happy.

I had left my wife and kids in the car, because I hadn't wanted to bring my entire family in the back door. Poinsot said, "Well, who are you here with?" I said, "Oh, with my family. We're actually staying across the street in that little hotel there." He replied, "Actually, I own that place now." We chatted awhile, and then he said, "I invite you and your family to come back for lunch tomorrow as my guests." And we did. We had planned on going back down to Dijon, but I said, "We're going back there for lunch!"

Everyone was delighted, and Chef Poinsot just kept bringing out dish after delicious dish. Then he went down to the cellar and brought up a fabulous pinot noir. He referred to me as an *ancien*, meaning an old one—an old crewmember, which was exactly what happened again when we went to Meursault, where I had worked *les vendanges*. We were driving through Meursault trying to find the Domaine Michelot vineyard, and I was looking left and right because all these old towns look identical in a lot of ways. I looked up and saw an old man step into the street. I hit my brakes, and as he crossed, I said, "That's M. Michelot, the winemaker I worked for!"

I pulled up a bit and said, "Monsieur Michelot?" And he said, *"Oui?"* I said, "M. Michelot, I worked for you, cutting grapes back in 1984 and '85." And he said, "Oh… I'm an old man. I've had so many people work for me that I don't remember them all."

"Well, I was the American guy."

"Ah, the American guy—yes, I remember you now!" Then he turned and yelled to the porch where his wife, Genevieve, was seated, "Genevieve! *Nous avons un ancien! Allez!* Genevieve, we have an old-timer coming in! Open the gates!" To me, he said, "I invite you and your family to come in for a wine tasting." So we all made our way down to the old part of the cave, including my two boys, who sat down to their first wine tasting.

Winemaker M. Michelot with John Moeller and sons
Alexander and Zachary in Meursault, France, in summer of 2004.

Thanks to my improved conversational skills, along with his exceptional patience, M. Poinsot and I worked very well together through the summer of 1985. Then, late in August, he startled me by saying, "You know, John, it's time for you to go."

I looked at Chef Poinsot and didn't know what to say. He continued, "You need to go out and see more of the culinary world. I'll write you a letter of introduction and give you a list of restaurants and chefs to visit."

He helped me understand how important it was to broaden my cooking repertoire while I was young, and he saw that I needed to make the most of my time in France.

HOTEL DE LA CÔTE D'OR

Basically, the letter that he wrote said, "Here I present this young guy who worked for me this summer. Please speak to him and give him a chance." I headed to the Côte d'Or region of Burgundy and started to work down his list. *Côte d'Or* means "hills of gold" and is named because of the magnificent color from the grapevines that cover the hills in every direction as far as the eye can see. I stopped in at the Hotel de la Côte d'Or. There I met with Bernard Loiseau, showed him the letter, and asked him if he was looking for anyone. He said, "The season is starting to wind down, but I could take on another *stagiaire (*trainee)." Immediately after that, he said, "*Je ne payer pas* (I won't pay you), but you can stay here and I'll feed you."

Room and board, and that was it, so I had to do some hard thinking. I needed money to survive, but the real reason for my journey to France was to work in a restaurant of this caliber, two-star Michelin striving to become three-star. As it turned out, it took ten more years before Chef Loiseau got that third star, but in 1984–85 when I was there, he was already a rising star — he was chef of the year in the *Gault Millau* magazine and had been written up in several other magazines. I asked myself, *Well, should I just suck it up and live cheap for a couple of months?* There's nothing wrong with that, everyone should do it once in a while, just to understand living within your means. I decided, "Let's give this a try." And so I accepted.

I had two weeks off between leaving the job at Chez Camille and when I needed to report to Chef Loiseau, so I decided to call Monsieur Michelot at the vineyard in Meursault and ask about working the grape harvest again. He welcomed me back, and as a "veteran," I got to stay at the house this time. The extra money I earned made a nice addition to the couple of hundred dollars my folks sent to me, and helped me get by while I worked at Hotel de la Côte d'Or.

After those two weeks in the vineyard, I started work at Bernard Loiseau's place at the beginning of October and worked there through April. This was a whole other grade of cuisine! It was astounding just to see the level of cooking and how many cooks were in the kitchen—how many people it took to do everything. I benefited from it, without a doubt. I learned how to work with ingredients I had never seen before, and I got to be a part of the restaurant's effort to achieve its three-star Michelin status.

It was very exciting to watch what was being done. The restaurant managers and the servers would come back to the kitchen with a ticket and say, "*Très soigné*," by which they meant, "This is for a very important guest." The chef de cuisine kept a small box in the kitchen. He'd take an index card, write on it what they were serving to that particular guest, and file it under his name, so whenever that guest came in, we never served him the same thing we'd given him before. At times a guest might say, "I'll be happy with whatever you'd like to prepare for me," so we'd look at the index cards, see what he or she had eaten the last time, and create something different. Learning how to treat VIP guests was a priceless experience for me.

One day, the President of France came in for lunch. I happened to be working the meat station, and I made the filet that went on his plate. I found that very exciting, little knowing that a couple of years later I would be cooking for presidents and heads of state every day! Loiseau's place was also where I came to fully understand the importance of impeccable presentation. If we were dicing a tomato, for example, the dice had to be perfectly square. All our cuts had to be precise and uniform, without compromise. Everything had to be just right—a tomato, a slice of onion, the chopped chives we might sprinkle on top of something, or a sprig of herb used as a garnish—everything exactly the same each time. We'd pick through a whole bunch to remove any second-rate ones and to make sure that we selected the one that was first-rate, the one worthy of being on the plate that was going to represent us when it went out to the customer.

I was becoming accustomed to French culinary tradition and ingredients and a way of life, spending eight or nine months at one restaurant and then moving on to the next. I was starting to realize what valuable experience I was accumulating. Each time, as I went to the next level, I could really see the difference in the quality of ingredients I was using.

It always comes back to the ingredients!

At Loiseau's, we worked mornings and evenings, took a break between 2:00 and 2:30 in the afternoon, and came back at 5:30 for the dinner service. One day, I came back into the kitchen a bit early. I was the first one there, and as I walked in, I smelled something and thought, *What in the world is that? I've never smelled anything like it in my life.* As I followed my nose all over the kitchen, it brought me over to a table that had a very small balsawood box—like a miniature crate—five inches by five inches, sitting on it. There was white paper inside it, and I moved it aside, and there sat the first fresh truffle I'd ever come across. It perfumed the whole room; you couldn't escape it—it was intoxicating. In that special moment, I had one of the best experiences you could ever have with a black truffle. I mean, here in the States, yes, I'd opened a few cans of truffles (we didn't even have frozen truffles back then). They were the only truffles I'd ever seen back in the early 1980s, and their quality was minimal. Nowadays, you can buy frozen truffles, and you can get fresh ones, too—they cost a fortune, of course. But that afternoon, walking into that kitchen and experiencing that aroma, I was in awe. It was a culinary first for me: to see a truffle in its raw state. I know now, of course, that using a perfect fresh truffle like that, instead of using a canned truffle, makes all the difference in the world. Superior-quality fresh ingredients inspire a chef to experiment, to reach out and create innovative new dishes.

It was fantastic to work with Loiseau, who used all of the local ingredients and transformed them into his interpretation of regional Burgundy cuisine. Escargot, for example. Usually, people open a can of snails, put some garlic butter on them, stick them in the shells, and everyone goes wild. At the Hotel de la Côte d'Or, local people would bring in boxes of *le petit escargot* fresh, and we cooked them from the raw state. We'd open up the refrigerator and find them stuck on the inside of the door. They were crawling out and trying to get away. I think they knew what was going to happen as soon as they started smelling the thyme and bay leaves. You can't produce quality like that when it comes from a can.

That *très soigné* VIP experience at Loiseau's was what I later recreated every single day at the White House, whether I was serving the President and the First Lady a casual dinner upstairs, or if the President of France was downstairs for a working lunch, or preparing a state dinner for the Prime Minister of Japan.

All in all, my progression through the restaurants, from bistro to Michelin, couldn't have gone better if I'd planned it. From beginning to end, it was absolutely perfect. And back in the States, it turned out that the whole French experience in general, and particularly my time at Loiseau's, was an important factor in finding work. Having VIPs come in there on a daily basis, I had to produce a first-rate product all the time. Everything that left the kitchen had to be perfect the first time out. There was no second chance. Absorbing that sense of commitment to such a high level of quality was invaluable in my development. Later, it was one of the deciding factors in my being brought on board at the White House.

I had been working with Chef Loiseau in Saulieu for just seven months when circumstances found me on the move again. An officer approached me as I was entering my car outside the restaurant one afternoon, and asked me in French, "What nationality are you?" He demanded my papers, looked at my passport, and saw that I had overstayed my visa, so he ordered me into his police van. We sat at a little table in the back, and he grilled me about what I was doing, why I was there, and what my plans were. Finally, the policeman wrote me up as an illegal and told me I had to report to the prefecture in Dijon the next day—some ninety kilometers away. Before making that drive, I tried to figure out what to do. I assumed I was going to have to move, but where? Then I remembered a friend, Jean-Yves Crenn, a chef from Cléder, in Brittany, near the English Channel.

Before I left for Loiseau's, he had told me, "If you ever need anything, give me a call." So I rang him up and said, "Hey, I think I'm in trouble here," and explained my immigration difficulties.

"Look," he responded, "my busy season is about to begin, and I could use some extra help, so just jump on a train and come up here." I agreed to give him a call after my trip to the prefecture.

The next day, I drove to Dijon and reported to the prefecture. The officer took me to an interrogation room and started grilling me all over again. He launched into a tirade—all in French—about how I had overstayed my visa and was working illegally. He went on and on, stressing how serious it all was. "Don't you know," he yelled, "I could throw you in jail—or put you on the next plane back to America?"

Finally, he stopped yelling. He looked at me like he was sizing me up, and continued in a calmer voice. "And you—what are your plans now?"

"Well, I'm planning to leave town." What else could I say?

"Okay, then," he warned. "But if I see you around anywhere, I'll have to take you into custody, and you'll be on the next plane back to America!"

I left the prefecture and immediately found a phone to call Jean-Yves up in Brittany. He reassured me, "Relax. Just come on up here."

I boarded a train for Cléder the next day, and was soon working at his restaurant, another small, but upscale, country restaurant—this time in Brittany.

Those six months introduced me to yet another style of regional cooking, further broadening my culinary repertoire, but I began to feel that (immigration troubles notwithstanding) it was time to head back across the Atlantic. My short backpacking trip to Europe had grown into a two-and-a-half-year odyssey! Without having a real agenda, I had lived day to day, barely aware of how much time had passed.

Looking back over those days—the people I met along the way, and the experiences and opportunities that presented themselves—I suddenly realized that I had accomplished my goals. My ambition had been to experience cooking in France and to earn credentials as a French chef. I knew that I was ready to move on and use what I had learned.

It was time to head back home to the United States.

A Reflection on
My French Experience

When I had returned to France, I had no plan. All I knew was that I was a chef, and I wanted something more. To be able to move up from what I call bistro-level cooking to a Michelin-type level was part of the Holy Grail; it was what I wanted to achieve.

I was lucky to have had this experience at a time when being a chef was becoming a profession here in the United States — when the job came of age, celebrity chefs were starting to emerge, and eating in general was elevated to a different plane. When I returned from France in 1986, I could see that chefs here were also starting to really take notice of the ingredients they were using; since that time, I've seen enormous changes in contemporary ideas about food.

Appreciation of Wine

Appreciation of wine was another thing that I learned from my time in France. Wine was already popular here in the States when I went over to France in 1984, but hadn't yet gone through the renaissance that it did during the late 1980s and '90s. Now, through my experience of living an everyday life with the French people for two years, working in the vineyards, and working in the various levels of restaurants, I had learned how to really taste wine.

It's because I went and actually handpicked the grapes and learned about them that I acquired an appreciation of the wine and came to understand how to choose wines to complement food. Once your hands touch it, and you're doing it and seeing it and living it, you have a whole different appreciation than just pouring a glass of wine and saying, "Oh, that tastes good. I like the chocolate overtones." and all that stuff. But whenever I look at a bottle of Meursault, for example, I think of those backbreaking days I spent picking the grapes out in the fields. Walking around the farm at night, I was curious, so I looked down into the cellar where they were starting to press the grapes. I just stood and watched, thinking, *So this is how they make wine*. It was thoroughly interesting. I never did have the chance to actually make the

"Yes. I wonder if you're looking for any chefs right now."

"Do you have papers?"

I handed him my résumé, and he disappeared into the kitchen. He returned with the chef, who introduced himself as Chef Jean Ruiz and asked how I'd heard about the Four Ways. To keep things simple, I answered casually, "Oh, I was just walking by."

Jean invited me to sit down in the bar with him as he looked over my résumé. As we discussed my background, I learned that he was French-Belgian and was familiar with some of the places in France where I'd worked. One in particular caught his eye: "Oh, you worked at Bernard's place in Saulieu!"

He knew Bernard Loiseau at the Hotel de la Côte d'Or in Burgundy.

"Man," he said, "I'd love to have you come work with me full time, but right now I only need a part-timer." He paused a moment, then said, "I'll tell you what: if you'll work with me through the rest of the summer, I'll give you the banquet-chef position in September when we get busy."

I didn't have to think long about this offer, so I accepted: "Sounds good to me!"

It seemed unbelievable—I'd been in Washington only a few hours. I had arrived after ten o'clock that morning, and by mid-afternoon I had a job! I left the interview and wandered out to the street. Across the way I noticed a little café with outdoor seating—it reminded me of France. I sat down at one of the tables for a sandwich and a beer. It was quiet, and I struck up a conversation with my waitress. I told her, "Jeez! I just got to town this morning, and I already landed a job—right over there." I pointed across the street. "Now I have to find a place to live."

She said, "Why don't you check that bagel shop across the street?"

The shop featured a community bulletin board where locals posted all kinds of announcements, including ROOM AVAILABLE notices, so I finished my lunch and took her advice. Among the bulletins was one that read "Sublet My Apartment for the Month of July." That made a lot of sense—if this thing at the Four Ways turned out to be a mess, I wouldn't be stuck with a long lease. I could head back to Lancaster and pick up where I'd left off. It wasn't a mess, however, and a month later I was looking for a long-term living arrangement. At summer's end, Jean kept his promise, and I moved to full-time work at the Four Ways.

A month into the job, Jean approached me after service one evening and asked, "What are you doing tonight?" I told him I had no plans, and he continued, "Why don't you come along with me? Now and then, all the French chefs in Washington get together. Tonight we'll gather at the Mayflower Hotel."

"Sure!" I replied. It sounded like fun. "Your French is good enough," he reassured me. "You'll have no trouble participating in the conversation."

When we arrived at the Mayflower, Jean introduced me around. Among the group was Pierre Chambrin of the well-known Maison Blanche restaurant. Neither of us knew that this meeting would turn out to be a milestone in my career path. Pierre was destined to become sous-chef at the White House a few years later.

My experiences in France and my ability to converse in the language gave me an inside track with that crowd. I really hit it off with several of the chefs—including one of the Mayflower chefs who had worked in Dijon. I knew the hotel and several fine restaurants where he had worked. I ended the evening as a new—if unlikely—member of that elite circle!

I continued to work at the Four Ways for nearly two years—till it ran into some financial difficulties and closed in the summer of 1989. I'd heard that Pierre Chambrin was looking for help, so I contacted him to let him know I was available, but we couldn't make it work. In fact, for months after I left the Four Ways, Pierre and I made several attempts to work together, but we were never able to make it happen. Then we lost touch for a while.

Someone told me that Pierre was working at the White House, but it was nearly a year before I heard from him again. Then one day my phone rang. "This is Pierre," he said. "What are you doing these days?" I briefly described my current situation, and then he said, "Well, I'm a sous-chef at the White House. They brought me on a year ago in anticipation of the executive chef retiring. They've been prepping me as a possible replacement. Now it looks like I've got the job—and I need to replace myself." And then, "Would you be interested?"

"Yeah! Let's meet and talk about it."

I was working downtown at that time, in the restaurant at the Westin Hotel (this later became the ANA, All Nippon Airways, and then the Monarch), so it was simple to arrange to get together after work one night. We decided to meet at Trader Vic's, the popular bar that used to operate at the Capitol Hilton. The two of us sat, had a drink, and chatted about the White House.

Pierre emphasized over and over, "It's a very special place. I don't even know how to describe it exactly, you know?"

He talked about the complex personalities you have to deal with. "It's not so much the president or the first lady—it's all the other characters who work in and around the White House. Cooking at the White House is different."

He made an important point: "It's not a restaurant; it's not a hotel. You're cooking in somebody's home—and you're serving them almost every single day."

As I was beginning to get a picture of what it meant to cook at the White House, he looked at me and said matter-of-factly, "You know, I'm French-born, and I've been an American citizen since 1977." (You have to be a citizen to work full time at the White House.) "There are only five full-time chefs in the kitchen, and two of us—myself and the pastry chef, Roland Mesnier—are originally from France."

Then he got to the heart of the matter: "I could bring in another Frenchman, but I think that would be too many French people. What I really need is an American who understands French cooking. I want someone like you, with your background and extensive experience in France."

Who could have guessed that my experience in France would turn out to be the biggest factor setting me apart from other candidates for the White House job?

When I agreed to submit my application, I had no idea what an ordeal I was signing up for. The process began with a phone call from the chief usher, who serves as the general manager for all White House operations. Chief Usher Gary Walters called me to schedule a personal interview, which went very well. At the end, Gary presented me with a serious load of paper, including a lengthy form headed "A Questionnaire for Sensitive Positions." Gary looked apologetic: "This is a lot of work, I know, but I need you to fill it out and get it back to me as soon as possible."

I worked like a dog on that paperwork for three or four days, trying to account for every place I'd ever lived and every job I'd held since my eighteenth birthday. I had to remember employers' names and find contact information for each of them. I was thirty years old and they wanted details from the previous twelve years, a period during which I had moved around a lot, including my time overseas. It was truly a relief when I could finally call the chief usher and report, "I've completed all the paperwork." He seemed surprised: "Oh, you have the paperwork done already? That's great."

I hand delivered my application at the White House East Appointment Gate. The guard called the ushers' office, and after a few minutes, Gary came out.

He thumbed through the pages and then, apparently satisfied, asked, "Do you have time right now to come in and talk some more?"

"Sure," I replied.

He led me into a little room called the Map Room. Pierre joined us, and we sat down to talk.

"We've reviewed everything," Gary said, "and we'd like to offer you the position." He told me about the salary range and some of the job requirements, and then asked, "Are you still interested?"

I smiled. "Yes, I'm still interested."

So he discussed more details about the job, including what still had to happen before I could start work. "As you might guess, we'll have to do a very thorough background check before your final approval. There will be some phone inquiries—the FBI will call you in the coming weeks."

To prepare me for what was yet to come, he continued to describe the process, and then concluded by saying that it would probably take the entire summer to complete the background check. They didn't expect to bring me on till September.

So there I was, receiving a firm offer around the first of June, and learning that I had to wait till September. That was a very long summer—waiting and wondering what would happen next. Could there possibly be anything in my past that would cause them to reject my application?

I didn't know what would happen when I went back to the Westin to tell my boss about my plans. I decided to be direct: "Chef, it looks like I have a new position, but the job won't start for at least a couple months."

After I explained the situation to him, he surprised me, saying, "Wow! That's fantastic! In fact, we're honored that one of our staff is going to work at the White House. Just keep me informed of your plans and how things are working out."

President James Buchanan was the 15th president, and is the only president to have come from the state of Pennsylvania. He was a bachelor and his niece, Harriet Lane, served as his official hostess at the White House. The beautiful china that he used as his dinnerware at the White House was manufactured by the French manufacturer, Sèvres.

President George H. W. Bush and First Lady Barbara Bush.
Courtesy George Bush Presidential Library and Museum.

President George H. W. Bush
and
Mrs. Barbara Pierce Bush
(1992–1993)

North Portico of the White House.
Courtesy George Bush Presidential Library and Museum.

First Family Welcome

It seemed strangely quiet when I arrived at the White House on September 18, 1992. It was "crunch time"—the last few weeks of George H. W. Bush's bid for reelection. I was a bit nervous as I approached the security checkpoint at the East Appointment Gate—especially as I presented my chef's toolbox with its array of knives. "We knew you were coming," said the guard, and he called Executive Chef Pierre Chambrin to come and escort me in, since I hadn't yet received a permanent pass. As we walked the path and I looked up at the majestic columns of the North Portico, it was hard to believe that I was really going to be working here—at the White House itself.

With everyone out on the campaign trail, that first week at the White House found me pacing like a caged animal—full of nervous energy but with nothing much to do. Even the weekend was quiet, as the First Family was at Camp David. We all tried to stay busy—doing prep work and looking at upcoming events. I'd heard that Christmas would completely dominate our daily schedule within a few weeks, but for now, the daily busywork seemed to expand and fill the time while we waited to cook for the President and the First Lady.

The slow pace during that week gave me too much time to think about my "debut," scheduled for the next week. The First Lady let us know that she had invited two guests for lunch, and Pierre assigned me the luncheon. If I'd caught the assignment on my first day, I'd have just taken it in stride: "Okay, we've got lunch for three at one o'clock." And I would have just done it. As it was, I had over a week to stew over the details. It was nerve-racking.

I started planning the menu, referring to a list of Mrs. Bush's likes and dislikes and what to avoid. I went over the menu with Pierre, who said, "Sounds good."

I had bought everything I needed to prepare the meal, and the day of the luncheon found me working all morning—starting in the main kitchen on the ground floor. For First Family dining, we did the "hard cooking," or major preparations, there, and we put on the finishing touches and served the meals from the residence kitchen on the second floor. I would set up that kitchen and turn on the ovens we needed forty-five minutes before the meal, then we'd transport everything up from the main kitchen and be ready to serve right on time.

The residence kitchen was considerably smaller than the main kitchen, and had a window with a view of Pennsylvania Avenue. I liked standing there and looking down at the tourists pouring out of buses and lining up to see the White House. I felt privileged to be on the inside looking out.

We were ready to go—plates for hot courses in the warming drawer, salad plates in the refrigerator—just waiting for the call from the First Lady. Pierre used the time to tell me what to expect, including the fact that meals don't always start promptly. "The First Lady sometimes stops in the kitchen to say hello or give some last-minute instructions, or she might go directly to the dining room. Once at the table, the butler might come back and tell us that she's ready—or she might buzz us."

Under the head of the table there was a button for the host to signal the kitchen for the next course or call us with a special request. When the buzzer sounded, it usually meant "next course," and we'd spring into action to get the service out. As Pierre explained these details to me, the butler entered the kitchen and told me, "The First Lady wants to see you in the dining room."

Time stood still for a moment. Nervously, I looked over at Pierre, then at the butler, and then back at Pierre, who was waving his arms as he said, "Well, go! Don't keep her waiting!" And I rushed out the door.

I entered the dining room and approached the First Lady for the first time. I hadn't met her during the interview process, and hadn't had to "try out" with a tasting menu. There'd been no introductions, so I felt a bit stunned to suddenly be in the presence of this very public figure. I had seen her in photos and on TV, of course, but here she was, seated in front of me, conversing with her luncheon guests. She looked up at me and said, "Oh! So you're one of our new chefs."

As I responded, "Yes, I am," she extended her hand. I shook it and said, "My name is John Moeller."

She looked thoughtful. "You know, you'll have to forgive me—I've been on the road a lot lately, but I think I've met someone from your family. I just can't remember exactly where."

"Really?" I replied, my mind racing to figure out whom that could possibly be. None of my family members had mentioned meeting Barbara Bush and telling her about me. I would certainly have remembered that! I didn't know quite what to say: "So … uh … well, what part of the country were you in? I have family in the Midwest, in Pennsylvania, and the Northeast."

"I've been in the Northeast," she said. "It might have been Connecticut or somewhere up there."

"How about New Jersey?"

Her face lit up. "Yes, I think it *was* New Jersey. We were having a little fundraiser luncheon with a group of ladies. A woman in the receiving line introduced herself and said she had a nephew who had just accepted a job as a White House chef."

A bell went off in my head. *Bingo! That has to be Aunt Irene!* She and my Uncle John owned a successful business in Bergen County, New Jersey, and were very strong Republicans. To Mrs. Bush I said, "That must have been my Aunt Irene. She lives in that area, and I'm sure she would have come to a special luncheon attended by you."

The First Lady apologized for not remembering all the details of her story. Then she changed the subject and asked about today's lunch menu. After describing it to her, I turned to go. I headed back to the kitchen in amazement. Meeting the First Lady was nothing as I imagined it would be. It was so relaxed, almost casual. She'd taken time from visiting with her guests to introduce herself to me, and remembered to tell me about meeting my aunt—unafraid to admit forgetting the details.

Her laidback attitude took me completely off guard, but by the time I reached the kitchen, I had shaken it off. We served the lunch without a hitch, and Mrs. Bush was pleased. In the short time that I served President George H. W. Bush and First Lady Barbara Bush, I came to appreciate their warm attitude toward us and how they maintained a very close relationship with the staff.

Those thoughtful, genuine feelings showed up in little details around the White House. For example, behind the West Wing, near the Oval Office, there was a horseshoe pit. Staff members were allowed to use it when they had time. If the President heard some clanging outside his window and could spare a few moments, he would step out through the patio and toss a few horseshoes with us. Good times in the White House backyard. One of the things that I came to appreciate throughout my years at the White House was that it's a family home, and the first families always treated us like family.

President Bush pitches horseshoes at the White House.
Courtesy George Bush Presidential Library and Museum.

On one occasion I mentioned to President Bush that my dad was the manager at the Lancaster Airport in PA and that the crew of the new Air Force One had presented him with a photo of the aircraft during one of their training sessions at the airport. I asked if he would sign it and he was only too happy to oblige.

Jan 7, 1993

To John Moeller —
Fly High, John, Just like AF I — Best Wishes,
G. Bush

Photograph of Air Force One presented to John Moeller's father by the
crew of Air Force One and signed by President George H. W. Bush.

When I arrived at the White House, Executive Chef Pierre Chambrin
managed the kitchen with the help of two sous-chefs. Pierre had been trained
in the classic style of French cuisine at École des Métiers de l'Alimentation in
France, and he had been brought in to the White House as a sous-chef early
in the Bush administration. The Bushes were very pleased with his work and
he was appointed as White House Executive Chef when Hans Raffert retired.
He assigned me the number-two position, and the third chef was next in line.

Pierre ran the show, of course, but he was primarily responsible for official
functions — state dinners, receptions, and other big events. That left the other
two of us to manage day-to-day operations and cover all the family meals.
When Pierre was working on an official event, whoever wasn't serving the
family would help him with his preparations. This arrangement gave me the

opportunity to get to know President George H. W. Bush and First Lady Barbara Bush. They were generous and considerate in their relationship with us, and that made it easier to serve them.

The First Couple were very well traveled and appreciated a wide range of fine foods. They liked everything we prepared, and didn't require us to submit menus for day-to-day dining. Pierre maintained a "Do/Don't List" and instructed us to abide by it. He emphasized being aware of recent menus and what was planned in the near future, but for the most part, the First Family would sit down to dinner each evening without knowing the menu in advance.

As long as I paid attention to the list and made sure we were providing variety and balance, I was free to try some different things. We had been experimenting with Asian cuisine at the restaurant where I worked before coming to the White House, and hearing that the President had spent time in Asia back in the 1970s, I decided to do an Asian-style dinner one night. I wanted to make sushi—not raw, but cooked—so I put together a Japanese menu that included teriyaki salmon and miso soup. And I brewed some green tea. The butlers were concerned about the tea. They told me, "You have to make coffee! They have coffee every—"

"Tell you what," I interrupted, "you make the coffee, and I'll have the tea ready. Just ask them what they want."

The butlers seemed scared of altering the routine. After doing things the same way over and over, they had let it become a rigid procedure not to be tampered with, and felt intimidated about making "unauthorized" changes.

Presented with a choice of green tea or coffee, the First Couple selected the tea. I have to admit that I rather enjoyed saying to the butlers, "Now, guys, that wasn't so bad, was it?"

After dinner, the President came back to the service kitchen. He shook my hand and said, "Ah, John, that was great! In the four years I've been here, I have never had a meal like that."

"Thank you, sir," I replied. "I appreciate that."

idea. At that point we were acutely aware that we served "at the pleasure of the President."

I did have the honor of meeting the first White House chef, René Verdon, in the late 1990s. He showed up at the White House one day while traveling to promote one of his books, and I was asked to give him a tour, since I was the only one available. I showed him, and the friend accompanying him, around the White House. We had a great conversation, and as I was showing them out, Verdon mentioned that they were headed to the Metro. It had been years since his last visit to Washington, and they seemed a little confused about how to get there. I still had a little time, so I just walked them over to the Farragut North Metro stop. I helped them buy tickets and made sure they got on the right train. A few weeks later, René sent me a nice thank-you note, along with an autographed copy of his book.

Making a Home in
a Historical Setting

The White House complex has over 67,000 square feet total (including the wings) and sits on more than eighteen acres of land. The residence alone covers 55,000 square feet. The two upper floors have 3,000 square feet for the first family's private living area. An incoming first family has to make a lot of decisions about furnishings, colors, fabrics, and carpeting—details that help make it feel like their place and leave their "stamp" on the facility.

Every first family since President John Adams and First Lady Abigail Adams has had this responsibility. In 1800, the second President and his wife became the first residents of the executive mansion when they moved in for the last six months of Adams's term. Only six rooms were actually habitable at that time. There's a painting showing Mrs. Adams supervising a servant hanging wet laundry in the unfinished East Room!

Not many years later, in August 1814, invading British soldiers burned the White House during the War of 1812, and chased President James Madison and his colorful First Lady Dolly Madison from Washington. After the war, it took from 1815 to 1817 to rebuild the burned-out mansion. I have heard that as late as the 1980s they would still find charred areas under layers of paint during maintenance and restoration projects. Stonemasons working on the exterior during my years told me about seeing evidence of the 1814 fire. In fact, some of the stone visible from the Truman Balcony on the south side was never repainted. You can clearly see burn marks there. President Clinton was fond of taking guests to see those charred stones. He used it as a visual reminder that the White House carries in its structure all the history of the nation.

On the ground floor of the residence is another area where we staff members could see some dark signs of the burning. Regular tourists aren't permitted into that area, but we would point it out for our occasional visitors: "Here are some of the original burn marks from when the British burned the White House in 1814."

DINNER

In celebration of
The 200th Anniversary
of The White House

Truffle and Duck Consommé
Roasted Vegetables and Madeira
Seared Striped Bass
Corn and Crab Fricassee
Chive and Oyster Sauce
Grapefruit and Gin Sherbet
Smoked Loin of Lamb
Heirloom Apples, Butternut Squash and Salsify
Terrine of Pears, Figs and Wild Ripened Cheese
Winter Greens
Fig Dressing
Abigail Adams' Floating Island
Raisin Biscuits
Lemon Bars

Kistler *Chardonnay* "Cuvee Cathleen" 1996
Landmark *Pinot Noir* "Kastania Vineyard" 1997
Bonny Doon "Vin Glaciere Muscat" 1999
The White House
Thursday, November 9, 2000

Dinner menu for the celebration of the 200th Anniversary of the White House.

Commemorative plate celebrating the 200th anniversary of the White House, with a place setting of the Clinton dining service.
Courtesy Lenox Corporation.

Through the years, as the government grew larger and more complex, the White House became more and more overcrowded. Before either wing was constructed, administrative offices were located near the private residence. President Roosevelt complained that he could hardly get any sleep with people running up and down the stairs all the time. Between the burgeoning government, Roosevelt's large family, and the addition of new developments like electrical and telephone wiring, the expansion was desperately needed. Finally, at the turn of the twentieth century, Teddy Roosevelt led in the construction of the West Wing, begun in 1902.

During the Truman years, engineers discovered that the White House interior was in danger of imminent collapse. The first family moved across the street to Blair House while the main residence was entirely gutted and rebuilt on the same design. They took this opportunity to develop the third floor of the residence. Previously, that level was used for storage and a few servants' bedrooms. The central and east areas of the third floor were developed into casual living space for the first family and six guest bedrooms.

SURROUNDED BY MUSEUM PIECES

Since the first family always ate their private meals in the dining room on the second floor, we spent a lot of time in the elevator each day as we took dishes, food, and supplies from the main kitchen two floors below. The elevator opens into a short passageway on the second floor, which is a busy place during meals, since the butlers use it while serving the family. Looking to your left after stepping off, you face the upstairs kitchen. In the opposite direction, you see a large pair of doors.

The double doors open into the West Sitting Hall at the west end of the private residence. If you go through the doors and look to your right, you'll see a large oil painting hanging there—Claude Monet's *Morning on the Seine, Good Weather*. It's on the north wall between the double doors and the west wall with its gigantic arched window. The plaque at the bottom of the ornate frame reads: "A gift to the White House in memory of John F. Kennedy." The Kennedy family donated it to the White House in 1963, and it has hung in that spot ever since. As first families came and went, the furniture arrangement and décor of the Sitting Hall might change, but the Monet never moved.

When it's busy, and you're focused on your work, you hardly notice your surroundings—especially after months or years working there, but once in a while you have a moment to catch your breath—perhaps while waiting for the first family to arrive for dinner. There you are, by yourself, and suddenly it strikes you: *Wow! That's an actual Monet—I could reach out and touch it if I wanted to.*

One day early on, one of the ushers, Chris Emery, offered to show me the private residence while the first family was away.

We toured the dining room, the bedrooms, and the bathrooms. Chris took me down the central hall and into the Yellow Oval Room, a big hall for entertaining. There's a large living room and master bedroom for the first couple, and several smaller rooms for children or other family members.

The White House | Second Floor

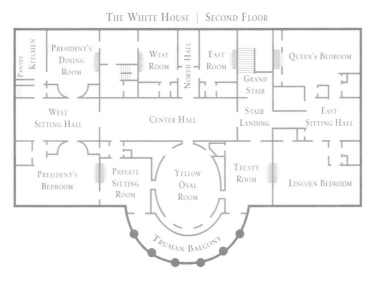

The White House | Ground Floor

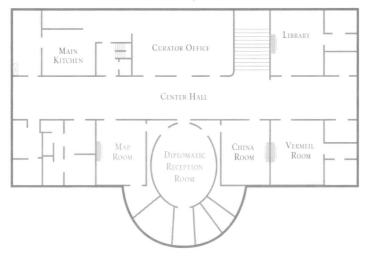

The Queen's Room and the legendary Lincoln Bedroom are at the east end of the residence, next to the Treaty Room where the president has his private study. When you step into the Treaty Room, the word "majestic" comes to mind. The nearly life-size presidential portraits, the ornate chandelier, and the massive ornamental mirror over the fireplace are overwhelming. The president uses this private study after hours or early in the morning. During the day he works at the Oval Office in the West Wing most of the time, but he might use the Treaty Room if he needs privacy or wants to have a quiet conversation with someone.

THE OVAL OFFICE

Since the navy took care of most of the food services around the Oval Office, we didn't work there very often, but I was able to step inside the famous room several times when the president wasn't around. A White House staff member or a Secret Service agent has to accompany all visitors. Inside the Oval Office, in addition to the president's desk, are pictures of family members and items the president finds inspirational. There are all kinds of little gifts brought to him by world leaders. You look around and suddenly it hits you: This is where history is made! You can almost feel the power.

At the end of each president's time in office, they disassemble and remove everything that was added to the Oval Office specifically for him. Then the National Archives Administration uses those items to construct a replica of his office at the Presidential Library and Museum constructed in his honor to house the papers of his administration. There is a library and museum honoring each president since Herbert Hoover, and most of them feature replicas of the Oval Office as it appeared during their individual administrations. The replicas contain authentic furniture and mementos, where possible, and accurate reproductions of permanent items that can't be removed from the White House.

Oval Office during the administration of President George H. W. Bush.

Courtesy George Bush Presidential Library and Museum.

Christmas at the White House

September 1992 started out very slowly for me. Since I was new on the job, I wasn't assigned much of a workload, but that was about to change — dramatically! Shortly after my arrival, I started hearing staff members discuss the coming Christmas season, and as the days went by, Christmas became the dominant topic of conversation — till it felt as if there was nothing else to talk about. I was certainly no stranger to the holiday season's importance in the hospitality industry — it's one of the busiest times of the year for hotels and restaurants — but it soon became obvious that a significant part of the White House social calendar revolved around Christmastime.

The White House holiday season actually begins on the first weekend of December with a party in honor of the annual Kennedy Center Awards. Then we would immediately shift into reception mode for the next three weeks. With as many as three receptions per day — averaging from 350 to 500 guests each — we'd serve some 20,000 people during those three weeks at Christmastime. On top of all those receptions — mostly for various government agencies — we had to serve special sit-down dinners for a variety of guests. Some were for senior staff, while others were thank-you parties for individuals or groups whom the administration wanted to acknowledge.

In July, there's a natural tendency to think you have plenty of time to worry about Christmas later, but selecting a theme and building a schedule of events takes a huge effort and, as December approaches, you see with your own eyes how much work goes into the holiday preparations. When the Clintons' first Christmas in the White House came around, I could sympathize with them when they saw the size and complexity of it. The social office needs input from the president and first lady early in the New Year because that's when we started planning Christmas. In January, the new president is just settling into the job, and someone walks up and says, "Time to start thinking about Christmas."

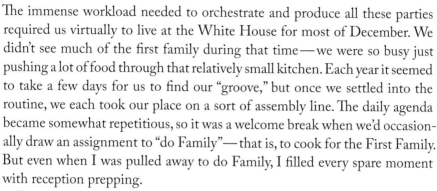

The immense workload needed to orchestrate and produce all these parties required us virtually to live at the White House for most of December. We didn't see much of the first family during that time—we were so busy just pushing a lot of food through that relatively small kitchen. Each year it seemed to take a few days for us to find our "groove," but once we settled into the routine, we each took our place on a sort of assembly line. The daily agenda became somewhat repetitious, so it was a welcome break when we'd occasionally draw an assignment to "do Family"—that is, to cook for the First Family. But even when I was pulled away to do Family, I filled every spare moment with reception prepping.

During those first Christmases, while Pierre Chambrin was still in charge, we maintained a decades-old tradition of producing large volumes of top-quality food. Over the years, the demands of serving these large gatherings had shaped the decision to serve familiar, hearty dishes—crowd pleasers. We didn't try to include salads or exotic delicacies; rather, it was more along the lines of "heavy hors d'oeuvres." We set up each reception as stationary service, spreading the tables so guests could serve themselves buffet style. Keeping the receptions more or less uniform made planning menus and managing events a little simpler. On the busiest days, receptions nearly overlapped, and if we over-prepared for one, we could use any excess food in the very next event.

Sheer volume prevented us from preparing little niceties like canapés or fancy appetizers. We kept busy making biscuits—sometimes 1,000 fresh biscuits every day! We prepared shrimp cocktails and platters of smoked ham and salmon. We set up several carving stations and went through countless filet mignons.

We produced barrels of eggnog—literally. We mixed the "high-test" libation in twenty-gallon barrels used exclusively for that purpose. We'd prepare five or six barrels in advance, and then use at least one per week through the rest of the season.

Our pastry chef, Roland Mesnier, had to start making Christmas pastries in August each year. Many of the holiday receptions featured pastries only, so he had to start early and work through September, October, and November to fill freezer banks of orange cakes and stamped cookies ready to bake. By Thanksgiving the freezer was jammed with pastries, but just three weeks later you could almost hear an echo in there because we were serving it all at an incredible rate.

Chef Roland Mesnier making White House Christmas decorations.
Courtesy George Bush Presidential Library and Museum.

Despite the large volume of pastries, Roland would not tolerate any decline in quality. For example, I remember his fruitcakes as perhaps the best I've ever tasted. Maybe it was because of all the alcohol he doused them with! Before wrapping them to pack away in the refrigerator, he would pour on straight brandy, allowing it to macerate for those months in the fridge.

All the food we prepared had to taste and look really good—and everything about the presentation had to fit with the season's decorating theme. Coordinating food presentations with flowers, decorations, linens, and presidential china is a constant priority at the White House, but Christmastime added a little more complexity to our event planning.

The White House is a beautiful establishment to begin with, but it undergoes a fascinating transformation for the holidays. Seeing this happen for the first time was a truly remarkable experience for me. The holiday makeover begins each year with the first family setting a decorating theme. Then, the head florist (at that time Nancy Clark) and the social secretary work closely with the family to come up with plans and designs for fleshing out the chosen theme. Finally, staff members carry out the actual decorating work, along with over a hundred volunteers. The volunteer decorators worked at the White House for up to five days. And that, of course, meant we had an additional 100 to 150 people to feed until they completed their tasks.

The volunteers would start their work at a support facility in Maryland, preparing the ornaments, garlands, and arrangements to be shipped to the White House. Then they came down to put it all together and hang the decorations. They moved through the State Level like a small army—magically transforming the State Dining Room, the Red Room, the Blue Room, the Green Room, and the East Ballroom. The Front Hall and Cross Hall were decorated lavishly as well. The Grand Hallway decorations would sometimes include up to a dozen trees reaching right up to the ceiling—taking up enough space to make you feel as if you were walking through a forest!

The residence floors were decorated as well, but not as extravagantly—and not by the volunteers. Only a few handpicked decorators and florists would handle the residence area. Not many people ever get a chance to see the first family's private residence, and those duties were entrusted only to full-time staff members who'd been there a long time.

White House Christmas decorations.
Courtesy George Bush Presidential Library and Museum.

The Best Christmas Party

As I watched layers and layers of parties unfold during the most intense weeks of my first White House Christmas season, I didn't fully appreciate exactly how everything worked. While the events weren't identical, there was a routine in the preparations and management from one to the next. The most interesting one turned out to be the last party of the season: the White House resident staff reception. That was *our* party. As with the other receptions, we made the preparations and set up the event, but at the party itself we were guests. Part-time staffers actually manned the reception, and they served us. It was especially impressive that first year to receive a personal invitation to a White House reception in the mail—in fact, it never grew old. It's pretty cool to take your family to a party at the most famous house in the world, even if you do work there!

Camp David

Shortly after the 1992 election, President George H. W. Bush asked the executive chef, Pierre, to put together a dinner party up at Camp David. Pierre invited me to plan the menu with him. "We'll treat this event like a catering gig," he said.

This would be my first of many trips to the presidential retreat. We created our shopping list, acquired the food, and did all the prep work we could in advance. The army always provided our ground transportation for these trips, which took an hour and a half to drive from the White House to Frederick County, in northern Maryland.

On the morning of the event, we packed everything we needed, and loaded the vehicle provided by the army for our trip to Camp David. It was a dreary winter day and particularly foggy. We drove up I-270 to the city of Frederick, then turned north on Highway 15 toward Thurmont.

At Thurmont we began to ascend Catoctin Mountain. The fog grew even thicker as we climbed up the east ridge of the Blue Ridge Mountains. Finally, a large unmarked gate appeared out of the haze and we pulled to a stop. Our driver identified himself, and the heavy gate opened, allowing us to proceed to a second gate. As we pulled forward, the first gate closed behind us, shutting us between the two. At the second gate our driver flashed his ID at a large surveillance camera. The name of each passenger in the car was verified against the guest list, and once security was satisfied, the second gate opened. The speaker crackled: "Okay, pull up to the checkpoint, and everyone exit the vehicle there."

At the checkpoint, we got out of the car and, as instructed, left the doors open. The marine security detail swarmed the car, opening the hood, the trunk, and every compartment for inspection. They examined the vehicle thoroughly, using flashlights to inspect the engine compartment, and mirrors to look underneath. Then the detail withdrew and gave us the okay to proceed. A short distance ahead we encountered a massive wood-frame gate towering above us in the fog. In the evening haze it looked remarkably like the main gate of Jurassic Park! It swung open automatically, finally revealing a sign: CAMP DAVID.

Enveloped as we were in dense fog under a gray sky, the whole place had a dreamlike feel. I looked around and could see a series of narrow path-ways — paved like golf-cart paths — winding off into the woods, but I couldn't see much that would help me get my bearings.

We drove down to Laurel Cabin. This is the building that houses the main dining hall, and it features a well-equipped professional kitchen as well. We pulled up, unloaded our supplies, and began to set up for dinner.

That evening, we served the President and First Lady and thirty or so guests a fine meal in the Laurel Cabin dining room. But thanks to the damp weather, I didn't see very much of the place. It was impressive just to be on the grounds of the famous retreat, but there was no way I could gain a full appreciation of it through that heavy fog.

We could just make out the president's cabin, Aspen Lodge, among the guest cabins along the winding pathways in the woods, but it wasn't till later visits that I got a good look at it. The cabin was beautifully decorated — luxurious yet rustic. It had a pool out back as well as a small practice golf hole that had a short fairway and a green with a couple of sand traps. In nice weather they would play golf, and call it a short par-three hole.

After we packed everything up, we called the army service to send our driver to take us back to Washington. Knowing it could take a little while for the car to get there, Pierre suggested, "Hey, let's go over to Shangri-La."

Shangri-La is Camp David's local "watering hole"—a bar located in Hickory Lodge, which also offers a pool table, a shuffleboard, a bowling alley, and even a little gift shop. The lodge provides a nice, informal place where the president and his guests can have a drink, hang out, and maybe shoot some pool. At one end of the building there's a small movie house. The president has access

Luncheon Menu *for the*
President *of the* Russian Federation:
November 2001

PUTIN LUNCHEON

The President of the Russian Federation, Vladimir Putin, made his first visit to meet with President G. W. Bush in November of 2001. The occasion was especially significant since it was only about four weeks since the 9/11 attacks.

In creating the menu, I chose to make a light lunch on this day because I knew we would be serving a Texas-style meal the next day at President Bush's ranch in Crawford, Texas.

LUNCHEON
IN HONOR OF HIS EXCELLENCY
VLADIMIR PUTIN
PRESIDENT OF THE RUSSIAN FEDERATION

ARTICHOKE AND LEEK SOUP
NANTUCKET BAY SCALLOPS

PAN-SEARED POUSSIN
CORN AND MOREL MUSHROOM CUSTARD
GREEN BEANS AND PEARL ONIONS
TARRAGON-SCENTED AU JUS

AUTUMN GREENS
PEARS AND MAYTAG BLUE CHEESE
TOASTED WALNUTS ～ MUSTARD SHALLOT DRESSING

HONEY AND TEA ICE CREAM
CHOCOLATE CAVIAR
WARM CARAMEL APPLES
LEMON SAUCE

GARY FARRELL CHARDONNAY "RUSSIAN RIVER" 1999

THE WHITE HOUSE
TUESDAY NOVEMBER 13, 2001

Menu card for Luncheon in Honor of His Excellency
Vladimir Putin, President of the Russian Federation.
November 13, 2001.

Artichoke & Leek Soup
with Nantucket Bay Scallops

Pan-Seared Poussin with Tarragon-Scented Au Jus, Corn & Morel Mushroom Custard, and Green Beans & Pearl Onions

*Autumn Greens, Pears & Maytag Blue Cheese
with Toasted Walnuts & Mustard Shallot Dressing*

President Clinton and Hillary Rodham Clinton stand alone at the
South Portico Entrance of the White House during the arrival
ceremony for King Juan Carlos I. February 23, 1999.

Courtesy William J. Clinton Presidential Library.

President William J. Clinton
and
Mrs. Hillary Rodham Clinton
(1993–2001)

President Clinton is inaugurated for his second term as President, as First Lady
Hillary Rodham Clinton and Chelsea Clinton look on. January 20, 1997.

Courtesy William J. Clinton Presidential Library.

that time. (I've heard that screening takes closer to six months since 9/11.) Rather than leave us to struggle shorthanded for months, Pierre graciously agreed to extend his "notice period" and stay on as executive chef till his replacement could be hired.

The media continued to buzz with news and rumors about who was on the list of candidates. They speculated on who would make the final cut. They interviewed well-known chefs to ask their opinions about who would be the new White House Executive Chef. At the same time, the White House got down to the business of interviewing chefs and inviting some to come in and do tastings.

My role in all this was to facilitate the process and assist the chefs who were unfamiliar with the White House. I made myself available to help with execution if needed, or simply to show them where things were in the kitchen. I hooked them up with the butlers who would help them get the needed plates, showed them the rooms where meals would be served, and helped them serve their tasting menus. I was supportive where needed; otherwise, they were on their own. A couple of the candidates wanted just to do their own thing—content to take over the second-floor kitchen and work alone.

Different chefs approached the tastings using their own methods. Most arrived with everything they needed, and with as much of the prep done as possible. Some brought their own food with them, so they could feel confident of the end result. The White House tastings required each chef to prepare a table for ten, and people from the social office would have the meal presented to them. Sometimes the President or First Lady was there, too.

Most tastings occurred midday, but the menu could be either a lunch or a more substantial dinner. Some chefs did their tastings as platter service, others brought in the food already plated.

A month into the process, I met Walter Scheib, the chef who eventually won the position. On arriving, Walter asked if I could show him around and help him out. We worked together to prepare the food and send it out. He was appreciative and seemed impressed with my willingness to help him. I believe he remembered that after they offered him the job and told him he could do whatever he wanted regarding his kitchen staff.

When Walter took over the kitchen in 1994, he interviewed both Sean and me. He decided to keep me, and replaced Sean with Keith Luce, a young chef who had previously worked with him at the Greenbrier Resort. Keith worked with us at the White House for almost two years. I was the only one left from the previous kitchen crew, so in 1994, barely into the second year of a new administration and with all the adjustments that had occurred, I now had to figure out my role with a whole new kitchen crew. How would Walter's management style differ from Pierre's? What did the First Family expect from us under a new executive chef?

Chefs Walter Scheib, Cristeta Comerford, and Jason Stitt
prepare dinner at Camp David. January 1, 1998.
Courtesy William J. Clinton Presidential Library.

It meant staying on my toes and being aware of everything around me. I kept my ears open and tried to anticipate what might happen next. Looking back, I feel good about my role in helping Walter assume his new position. From the outset, I made sure he understood that I had not applied for the position of executive chef and that I was there to support him. I assured him that above all I wanted us to get past all the anti-French business that had surrounded Pierre's last year. Working with Walter when he was doing his tastings had gotten us off to a good start. My attitude was "Let's just put all that stuff behind us and cook!"

So we set our sights on cooking, and making the President and First Lady as happy as possible. And we did a good job: Mrs. Clinton was very happy. She liked Walter's style and the new direction his menus brought. Things calmed down and stayed that way throughout the remainder of the Clinton years.

When Keith Luce left in 1995, Walter hired Philippine-born Cristeta Pasia Comerford, another young chef working in Washington, DC. She did very well, and in 2005 went on to replace Walter as executive chef during the George W. Bush administration. Cris was retained again by First Lady Michelle Obama, and continued as executive chef when that administration was reelected in 2012.

Walter brought a lot of new ideas—a fresh perspective and a new style. His "American-fusion" cooking style fitted perfectly with what the First Lady wanted to develop, and she was pleased. I remember her coming down to the kitchen after our first dinner with Walter to applaud him. Really! She clapped her hands and said, "This is the style I've been looking for!"

Keeping a first family happy sometimes resulted in sweeping changes. Another major change during the Clinton administration was in the style of our banquet service. From the time of the Kennedys—and likely before that—White House chefs presented the food at large functions platter-style. Guests were seated at tables of ten, with a designated "host" for each table. The host was someone who'd previously attended an official White House function and understood how our platter service worked. In the service at many banquets, the server holds the platter and places the portions on the individual guests' plates. However, at the White House, we presented each platter to each guest to serve himself or herself. For first-time guests, this could be intimidating. They would hesitate and wonder, *Am I doing this right?*

Poached Maine lobster
in fresh mayonnaise sauce.

A dinner platter of Tenderloin of Beef, Cremini Mushroom Sauce,
Chestnut Spaetzle, Glazed Root Vegetables, and Broccoli.

Our butlers would take the platter to each table's host, so the host could
demonstrate what was supposed to happen. The rest of the guests could
watch and follow suit, as the butler presented the platter to each in turn.
Often, the first platter would have both the meat portions and the starch or
a vegetable. Right behind it would be a second platter with the rest of the
main course—whatever didn't fit well on the first platter. To complete the
main course, there might be a gooseneck with sauce for each guest to ladle
onto his or her plate as desired.

We would occasionally vary how we served the soup and salad before the main course. Sometimes the butler would ladle the soup from the terrine into the guests' bowls; other times the guests served themselves. Salad was usually presented in a large silver bowl for the guests to make their own selection.

A platter of Tenderloin of Beef in a Texas Marinade; Spinach and Sweet Potato Batonnets; Spring Vegetable Ragoût for the Dinner honoring the Governors of the States and Territories, February 27, 2005. This was one of the first large events for which John Moeller catered as acting White House Chef.

A presentation of spectacular White House dessert platters.
Courtesy Chef Roland Mesnier.

Desserts were also presented on platters. Our pastry chef, Roland Mesnier, did a fantastic job creating beautiful dessert platters. He was pastry chef most of the time I worked at the White House, and I don't think he ever duplicated a dessert menu for an official function.

We paid special attention to the "*wow factor*" when constructing our platters. Each presentation was arranged and garnished to make sure it was glamorous—memorable. We wanted to impress every guest with the idea "*This is the White House!*"

The new President and First Lady decided they'd prefer a plated service at official functions instead of the traditional platter service. When they told

Walter to make that change, we were happy to accommodate—but we had to adjust our whole operation downstairs. Something as simple as "plating up" individual plates instead of platters forced us to take another look at our equipment and space requirements. We could put ten loaded platters in a warming oven, ready to go to the dining room and serve one hundred guests, but we could fit only thirty-five individual plates in each oven, so we needed at least three times as many warming boxes to take care of the same number of guests.

Then there was the noise factor. Every time you handle a metal plate cover, you risk a "clang!" With plated service, we tripled the number of metal covers—and the clanging. In the White House, we were often handling the food just a door away from the dining area, so we had to be extra careful not to make too much noise in the kitchen. We managed to work through the details, and the President and First Lady were very pleased with the results.

John Moeller moving food in a warming cart to a setup area in the Red Room. Carpeting was often rolled back to avoid any damage from the wheels. It was always important to take extra care when moving equipment around in the White House—which is like moving around in a museum.

We continued to make changes and adjustments as requested by the First Lady. Our big buffets, like the Christmas receptions, had previously relied on stationary displays for service. Now they wanted us to do more platters of canapés, served by butlers circulating among the guests. This affected more than the butlers: A typical event required six different items per guest. On a busy day with a couple of 500-guest receptions, we might need to produce 8,000 canapés. It was very labor intensive to assemble so many canapés quickly, so they could be served fresh, but we did it — and they were happy. And when the President and First Lady were happy, we were happy, too.

Chef Walter Scheib and the White House Kitchen Staff prepare hors d'oeuvres in The Old Family Dining Room. December 7, 1997.
Courtesy William J. Clinton Presidential Library.

All of these service changes really served as a sort of backdrop for the more fundamental changes in White House cuisine. That change was dramatic. Pierre Chambrin was a great chef — classically trained in French cooking. He knew his trade very, very well! His thick accent and his traditional French cooking style had created a special culinary atmosphere.

Walter entered the scene with a new cuisine. His repertoire reflected what was happening across the country throughout the 1980s and '90s — a kind of American food revolution. I had been watching this dramatic change firsthand. Having been in commercial kitchens since 1976, I saw the old-school style give way to chefs venturing into new ingredients and experimenting with different flavors to create something fresh and interesting.

Walter didn't just follow the latest fad — like a prosciutto-and-melon side dish or copying the latest popular entrée served with truffle sauce. He was somewhat adventurous, changing things up a bit and deliberately working with seasonal ingredients. We experimented with Asian cuisine, using Oriental and Indian spices and flavors, and there was an emphasis on regional produce, such as rockfish from Maryland.

As you might expect, after Walter arrived, we were inundated with suggestions and offers from all over the United States. Everyone, it seemed, wanted their products in the White House, but White House policy prohibits any specific product endorsements. We searched out great local and regional ingredients and purchased them when they were in season. It was exciting and fun to work within a philosophy that allowed us to try just about anything — within reason, of course. We understood the parameters of our freedom. We learned what the Clinton family did and did not like.

They preferred lamb to beef, for example, so we served a lot of lamb during those years. We'd prepare a rack of lamb or a chop and vary the cooking approach, the type of sauce, or the garnishes. It was innovative — sort of making it up as we went along. Most of the time we just worked in our own little world and had no idea if we were keeping up with the culinary industry or were at the leading edge. We didn't have that much contact with chefs across the profession, and seldom heard what others were working on or what was popular here and there. Consequently, we just created our own style as we worked out our direction with the First Lady. We had our own version of "American cuisine," and it was working very well.

Walter liked doing creative things with a lot of vegetables, which made it easier for me to execute my role as the First Family's dietitian. Not only did the family dining maintain a healthy balance, but the meals at official events also reflected a greater health consciousness. As vegetables assumed a greater role, we found that vegetable garnishing started consuming the largest part of our workdays. Cutting and searing meat and making the sauces were easy;

the tougher work involved preparing all the vegetable accompaniments to complement the meats. We spent a lot of time experimenting with combinations and making attractive presentations. And I enjoyed expanding my own culinary repertoire of recipes.

As you look at the menu cards in this book, you'll see the broad range of styles we covered, but what you'll see represents just a fraction of the menus from that era. To publish them all would require several volumes of nothing but menus, and even if you could examine every menu, you'd be hard-pressed to find two identical ones.

The selection of menu cards on these pages show the style and variety of menus served at the White House.

Luncheon

On the occasion of
The Signing of the Israel-Palestinian
Interim Agreement

Pheasant and Wild Mushroom Consommé

Broiled Salmon with Black Peppercorn and Ginger
Potato and Celeriac Purée
Parsley Sauce

Mesclun Salad with
Leeks and Beets
Walnut Vinaigrette

Black Raspberry Sorbet
Candied Strawberry Mousse
Macaroons

HAGAFEN "Reserve"
Chardonnay 1991

THE WHITE HOUSE
Thursday, September 28, 1995

LUNCHEON

Honoring His Excellency
The Prime Minister of India

Herbed Pasta Leaves with Asparagus and Fresh Morels
Roasted Tomato Coulis

Fillet of Copper River Salmon and Turbot
Napa Cabbage with Spring Vegetables
Saffron Basil Infusion

Young Spinach and Endive Salad
Grain Mustard Dressing
Phyllo Crisps

Mango Sherbet with Honey Sauce
Lime Compote
Cookies

THE WHITE HOUSE
Thursday, May 19, 1994

DINNER

Honoring
Mr. Nelson Mandela
President of the Republic of South Africa

Layered Late Summer Vegetables
with Lemongrass and Red Curry

Halibut with Sesame Crust
Carrot Juice Broth

Bibb Endive and Watercress
with New York Wild Ripened Cheese

Granadilla Sherbet
Lychees and Raspberries
Apple Sabayon
Cookies

JOSEPH PHELPS Viognier 1993
PETER MICHAEL Chardonnay 1991
PIPER SONOMA Tête de Cuvée 1985

The White House
Tuesday, October 4, 1994

DINNER

In honor of
Their Majesties
The Emperor and Empress of Japan

Seared Breast of Quail
White Corn Custard & Grilled Vegetables
Tomato-Cumin Sauce

Grilled Arctic Char and Lobster Sausage
Wild Mushroom Risotto
Braised Fennel
Vegetable Ragout
Roasted Garlic and Lime Sauce

Field Greens with Goat Cheese and Basil in Phyllo
Port Wine Dressing

Cherry Sherbet with Almond Ice Cream
California "Berkeley" Cherries
Wild Strawberry Sauce
Sushi Basket

KISTLER "Sand Hill" Chardonnay 1992
DOMAINE DROUHIN Oregon Pinot Noir 1992
ROEDERER ESTATE "Extra Dry" White House Cuvée

THE WHITE HOUSE
Monday, June 13, 1994

LUNCHEON

Honoring His Excellency
Antonio Guterres
Prime Minister of Portugal

Roasted Monkfish
Mushroom and Chorizo Risotto
Saffron Mussel Jus

Double Lamb Chops
filled with Roasted Garlic
wrapped in Swiss Chard
Spring Vegetables

Baby Romaine Salad
White and Purple Asparagus
Hazelnut Oil and Marjoram Dressing

Spring Crêpes Cake
Orange Sauce
Crème Fraîche

BRICK HOUSE "Estate"
Chardonnay 1995

THE WHITE HOUSE
Thursday, April 3, 1997

DINNER

Honoring His Excellency
The President of the Russian Federation
and Mrs. Yeltsin

Ginger Marinated Salmon
Cucumber Salad and Kasha

Rack of Lamb
Apricot Cardamom Chutney

Romaine and Watercress in Asiago Crisp
Grain Mustard Dressing

Lime Ice Mold
Berries and Peaches
Cookies

DEHLINGER Reserve Chardonnay 1992
WILLIAMS SELYEM Rochioli Vineyard Pinot Noir 1990
IRON HORSE Demi Sec 1989

The White House
Tuesday, September 27, 1994

Entertaining at the White House

Only two American presidents were younger than Bill Clinton when they took office. The fact that both Mr. and Mrs. Clinton were a lot younger than any first couple since the Kennedys had a definite impact on White House entertaining. Some observers even compared the Clinton White House to the "Camelot" days of JFK's administration.

The State Dining Room has space for thirteen tables of ten guests each, so for as long as anyone could remember, state dinners had been considered "at capacity" at 130 guests. Once in a while we had to accommodate a few more—say 140 or 150—but to do that, we had to open the big mahogany doors and seat the overflow in the adjacent Red Room.

The Clintons wanted to expand state dinners beyond the traditional number of guests. Their guest lists began to include more people than we could fit in the dining room. To accommodate larger gatherings, we set up the ground floor to serve drinks, dessert, and coffee for another sixty to eighty guests. After dinner, both groups would come to the East Room on the State Level to enjoy performances by notable artists. When configured for these performances, the East Ballroom could handle audiences of over 200.

The social secretary and her team stepped back and took a fresh look at these large events. What if we just served the dinner in the East Room? We could set tables for 240 in one room, or 200 if there was a performance stage. By moving our big dinners down to the East Room, we could serve everyone invited to a state dinner—at the same time, in the same room.

They continued to think creatively about how to accommodate large groups. In the months when the weather allowed, we'd move outside. They erected large tent pavilions on the South Lawn in which we could host picnics or dinners. We even did some very large state dinners under the tents—with four to six hundred guests. One of the last dinners we did at the Clinton White House was in honor of India's Prime Minister, Atal Bihari Vajpayee, in December 2000. We served 700 guests that night. Serving that many people outdoors in December was risky business, but since we had no choice, we figured out how to pull it off. An event that size could easily require over 2,000 plates, plus flatware and glasses. We had nowhere near that much service in-house, so we had to rent dishes for such large events. We needed to increase our equipment, too; for example, we acquired a portable walk-in refrigerator box that could be set up and powered almost anywhere on the grounds.

We learned not to lead with a hot course for these large outdoor events, but to serve the first course room temperature or cold, and follow with a hot entrée. Depending on the size of the event, we'd scale our production to make sure that everyone ate at the same time. You don't want the first guests wondering where the next course is before the rest have received their food. To time our service and get everyone served quickly, we designed a system of "satellite" kitchens, and sent food in from tents set up on both sides of the main dining area, which allowed us to handle very large numbers of guests.

These outdoor events didn't necessarily take place right next to the residence. Sometimes they'd set up giant tents in the lower area beyond the South Lawn, quite a distance from the buildings. That made transporting the food even more challenging. To move food that had been prepped in the kitchen, we used rolling carts, and had to roll them over some very bumpy cobbled walkways to the big driveway that encircled the South Lawn. We rolled downhill all the way to where the pavement ended, and then across some plywood laid down over the grass. It was always a challenge to transport all the food safely from the kitchen to the pavilions. At times the weather didn't cooperate, or some other complication made it tough, but we always managed, and the outcome was always great. Walter really enjoyed these massive events—he had a real gift for orchestrating and executing large functions. As executive chef, events were one of Walter's major responsibilities. These projects required more office time, more meetings, and an exceptional amount of planning. It was like catering on a massive scale, and while I was happy to help him in any capacity, I was even happier not to have his responsibilities.

Yes, at the White House we were always serving a real family in a real home—but much of the time it was also like working in a country club with a busy banquet facility. We catered event after event—breakfasts, lunches, dinners, and receptions, small or massive, indoors or out. It was like living a double life: we served in a family home one hundred percent of the time

Scenes from the Congressional Picnic held on the South Lawn in 2005.

Scenes from the Congressional Picnic held on the South Lawn in 2005.

while simultaneously planning and executing formal events at least ninety-five percent of the time.

President Clinton, a musician himself, had a younger taste in music and entertainment than his recent predecessors. His adopted theme song was *Don't Stop*, a rock hit by Fleetwood Mac. Beginning with Fleetwood Mac's appearance at the Clinton Inaugural Ball, the entertainment calendar at the White House had a new rock 'n' roll feel. The inaugural was only the first of Fleetwood Mac's appearances for the Clintons. VH1 hosted a couple of concerts on the South Lawn, as well. We were hearing a whole different kind of music around the White House. Walking through the house one day, I heard music playing outside: the Bob Dylan classic *All Along the Watchtower*, famously covered by Jimi Hendrix. I stepped outside to see who was playing, and when I peeked inside the pavilion, there was Lenny Kravitz playing guitar—with Eric Clapton. Stevie Wonder was there, too.

We not only had a chance to hear a lot of great talent perform at the White House but also got to meet a number of them face-to-face. It seemed that when celebrities were offered a VIP tour of the White House, they all wanted to see the kitchen. It was common while cooking to look up and see someone like Lenny Kravitz or Anthony Hopkins or members of famous bands like Aerosmith or the Rolling Stones. The day that Lenny and his entourage visited, I was impressed by what a great, down-to-earth guy he was. We had a friendly conversation before he moved on. Steven Tyler and fellow Aerosmith member, guitarist Joe Perry, also came through one day.

Occasionally, celebrities whose tour schedules brought them to Washington would receive an invitation to visit the White House. The Rolling Stones were once offered a private tour while they were in town for a performance. We were notified that they'd be in the house around three o'clock one Saturday afternoon. As we were waiting around to see which members of the band would actually show up, we suddenly heard someone playing the piano up in Cross Hall. It was Mick Jagger. I remember looking around to see if I could spot Keith Richards, but someone said, "He's not up yet."

When Anthony Hopkins showed up in my kitchen, he was full of questions, curious about the kitchen and its equipment. I remember being surprised that he only came up to my chin. When you see these stars on the big screen, you get the impression that they're much taller than they actually are.

Onlookers Sarah Farnsworth, Carolyn Huber, and John Moeller watch as Paul Newman puts the final touches on his snacks for Movie Night at the White House.

Joe Perry was accompanied by his wife Billie. As they looked around, her attention was drawn to the pots and pans hanging above. "Oh, those are nice copper pans! Do you use them a lot?"

"Oh, yeah," I answered, "all the time." I explained that they were copper on the outside, but that the inside was lined with nickel-steel.

"I really love those pans," she continued. "Where can I find pans like that?"

"Well," I said, "a lot of these pans are European—they've been here a long, long time. They've been part of the White House kitchen for many years."

Billie really was very interested in finding some good pans like the ones we had. I told her, "You know, I used to live and work in Europe. There was this great shop in the Les Halles area of Paris where professional chefs go to buy kitchen utensils and equipment. If you ever get to Paris, that's the place to find the best cooking equipment."

The Les Halles area has many shops that specialize in high-end cooking gear. The shop I recommended to her was full of all kinds of pans, utensils, and more. A chef could go crazy in there—just drooling over everything! The store isn't fancy—its merchandise is just piled high in stacks all over the place, even in its basement. Billie brightened a little: "Well, we're on tour now, but we plan on going to Paris this summer. What's the name of this store?"

I couldn't remember the name of the shop, so I offered, "Give me just a minute, and I'll find it." I went to get a little binder that I kept notes in from my time in France, looked up the name and address, and wrote them on a piece of White House stationery. I don't know if Billie ever made it to that shop, but she left very pleased that day, and I felt good about sending her on her way with some useful information. This was one of the fun parts of my job.

It's funny that people visiting the White House—a national monument full of drama and history—would want to see the kitchen. Of course they saw the well-known areas like the Red Room, the Blue Room, and the Green Room, but members of the Secret Service—who always helped out with VIP White House tours—said that the guests always asked to see the kitchen. It was something the average tourist couldn't see, which made it something of a mystery—a peek behind the scenes. Nearly every one of them would step into the kitchen and say something like, "This is it?" They were incredulous at how small the kitchen was—not more than thirty by thirty-five feet.

We stored most of our food in the basement under the North Portico. We had a couple of walk-in coolers where we kept refrigerated goods, a storeroom for dry goods, and a big freezer. We spent a lot of time going up and down that hallway because space in the kitchen was so limited. Most people are curious about food and how it's prepared, and getting to see the White House kitchen and learn about how we worked just added to a celebrity's feeling that he or she was getting special treatment.

As White House staff, we were allowed to bring our own guests for private tours just about any time. We could clear up to four people at a time for admittance to the facility, and we could show them around personally. It was great fun—and we always included the kitchen. It was a nice little perk, but I have to admit that it could get a little cumbersome at times. You'd be surprised how many times someone I barely could remember would suddenly think, *Hey, I'm going to call John and see if we can get into the White House!* Turns out, I had more friends than I ever realized! Mostly it was just fun. We made a lot of ordinary people feel special for a couple of hours.

ON THE ROAD

Almost all of our work took place in the White House itself, on the White House grounds, or at Camp David. During the Clinton years, however, the White House kitchen provided food services for two major events that were held far outside the Beltway: the First Summit of the Americas in Miami, Florida, and the Twenty-Third G8 Summit in Denver, Colorado.

THE FIRST SUMMIT OF THE AMERICAS IN MIAMI, FLORIDA

The Miami summit, held in December 1994, brought together heads of state from the thirty-four members of the OAS (Organization of American States) and their spouses.

We had responsibility to cater for this three-day event, a multifunction affair with lunches and meetings for the delegates and separate events for their spouses. We stayed at the Biltmore Coral Gables Hotel, but had to plan and coordinate simultaneous events at other venues as well, so we divided the work among us.

Once again, we found ourselves watching history unfold. This was the first Summit of the Americas, a gathering of the heads of state of the Western Hemisphere at which leaders discuss common issues and new challenges facing the Americas. Subsequent summits have been held in Chile, Canada, Mexico, Argentina, Trinidad and Tobago, and Colombia. The summit culminated in a big dinner for all the heads of state and their spouses at an exclusive residence on Fisher Island, a small island between Miami Beach and Virginia Key. We took a little ferry out to the island and executed the dinner in the resort's clubhouse kitchen.

There are many top-notch culinary professionals in South Florida, so the First Lady and the social office certainly could have used local services to prepare the lunches and dinners in Miami. But they wanted to demonstrate how important this summit was in the eyes of the United States. Bringing the White House chefs to Miami was a way of saying, "This is a historic event."

Also, Mrs. Clinton wanted to showcase the style we offered at the White House. She had tremendous confidence in Walter, and he came through with flying colors.

The First Lady's confidence in her White House chefs paid off in other ways, too. We already knew what she and the social office were looking for. Our attention to detail goes beyond that of most food services, and we are experienced at serving visiting dignitaries. We work with powerful public figures on a daily basis—at events ranging from intimate working lunches to grandiose state dinners with all their fanfare. We know how to deal with foreign embassies to ascertain the dietary needs and preferences of visiting dignitaries. An outside caterer wouldn't usually have any idea how to do that, so the responsibility would fall back on the social office. Our experience made it easier for them to rely on us for a lot of details required for an event of this kind.

President Clinton thanking John Moeller, Franette McCulloch,
and Walter Scheib at Vizcaya mansion in Miami, following an
event for the First Summit of the Americas in 1994.

DINNER

On the occasion of the
Summit of the Americas

Florida Lobster and Chanterelle Ravioli
Curried Key Lime and Coconut Sauce

Herb and Pepper Crusted Lamb with Creole Sausage
Chayote and Potato Crisp
Eggplant and Tomato "Martinique"
Roasted Bell Pepper and Garlic Sauce

Baby Romaine and Endive
Grilled Vegetables in Asiago Crisp
Sherry Vinaigrette

Apple and Mango in Phyllo   ·   Assorted Florida Fresh Fruit
Chocolate and Passion Fruit Log with Fresh Raspberries
Mocca Walnut Cake · Chocolate Mousse Cake · Sour Cherry Pie

BYRON Estate Chardonnay 1992
SILVERADO Cabernet Sauvignon 1986
MUMM Cuvée Napa Brut Prestige

THE VANDERBILT MANSION
FISHER ISLAND
Saturday, December 10, 1994

Menu for a dinner on the occasion of the Summit of the Americas held at The Vanderbilt Mansion, Fisher Island, Florida on December 10, 1994.

Another benefit of using the White House staff is that our high-level security clearance took a load off the Secret Service and other specialists who would have to check out and clear any outside help. They probably uttered a sigh of relief, knowing that our people were overseeing the production of all the food being prepared for thirty-four heads of state! I remember hearing about an attempted coup in South America some years back. Revolutionaries disguised as waiters suddenly took over the whole palace during an official dinner. You have to be able to trust the people who prepare and serve food for political leaders, so the White House had the confidence of using their regular team, and could vouch for us to the visiting dignitaries.

THE TWENTY-THIRD G8 SUMMIT IN DENVER, COLORADO

In 1997, the United States hosted the historic Twenty-Third G8 Summit in Denver, Colorado. Russia gained membership that year, thus turning the "Group of Seven" (G7) into a "Group of Eight" (G8), and it was Russian President Boris Yeltsin's first time to participate as a member. As heads of state from eight of the largest economies in the free world gathered with their spouses, we were essentially called upon to reprise our Miami performance. Unlike the summit in Miami, however, the G8 Summit didn't have a central hotel location. The meetings took place in the renovated Denver Central Library building, and we were provided a centralized kitchen to do prep work at another site.

We worked in "catering mode," doing our main prep in that kitchen, and then transported our product to various venues scattered around the Denver area. We served several events at The Fort, a fine restaurant southwest of Denver near Red Rocks Park, a forty-minute drive from the city. This is a beautifully

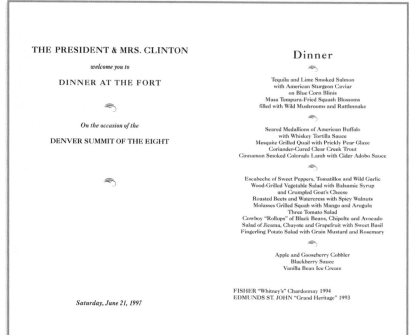

THE PRESIDENT & MRS. CLINTON

welcome you to

DINNER AT THE FORT

On the occasion of the

DENVER SUMMIT OF THE EIGHT

Saturday, June 21, 1997

Dinner

Tequila and Lime Smoked Salmon
with American Sturgeon Caviar
on Blue Corn Blinis
Masa Tempura-Fried Squash Blossoms
filled with Wild Mushrooms and Rattlesnake

Seared Medallions of American Buffalo
with Whiskey Tortilla Sauce
Mesquite Grilled Quail with Prickly Pear Glaze
Coriander-Cured Clear Creek Trout
Cinnamon Smoked Colorado Lamb with Cider Adobo Sauce

Escabeche of Sweet Peppers, Tomatillos and Wild Garlic
Wood-Grilled Vegetable Salad with Balsamic Syrup
and Crumpled Goat's Cheese
Roasted Beets and Watercress with Spicy Walnuts
Molasses Grilled Squab with Mango and Arugula
Three Tomato Salad
Cowboy "Rollups" of Black Beans, Chipotle and Avocado
Salad of Jicama, Chayote and Grapefruit with Sweet Basil
Fingerling Potato Salad with Grain Mustard and Rosemary

Apple and Gooseberry Cobbler
Blackberry Sauce
Vanilla Bean Ice Cream

FISHER "Whitney's" Chardonnay 1994
EDMUNDS ST. JOHN "Grand Heritage" 1993

Menu for dinner at Le Fort restaurant on the occasion of the Denver Summit of the Eight, Denver, Colorado. June 21, 1997.

situated restaurant in the hills facing eastward toward Denver proper. The view from the property — especially the large dining-room windows — affords an exquisite panorama of the foothills, which stretch out as far as the eye can see.

Menu for luncheon on the occasion of the Denver Summit of the Eight, Denver, Colorado. June 21, 1997.

This was also the site of our climactic final dinner on the last night. The weather allowed us to serve it — a western cookout served buffet style — on the terrace. We each worked various stations featuring a variety of grilled meats. At one point, President Clinton came by my station to get some meat. "Hey, John," he greeted me. "I hear we have elk here."

I was preparing some double-cut Colorado lamb chops on my grill, and I pointed to another station. "No, Mr. President, we don't have elk — but we do have bison on that grill over there."

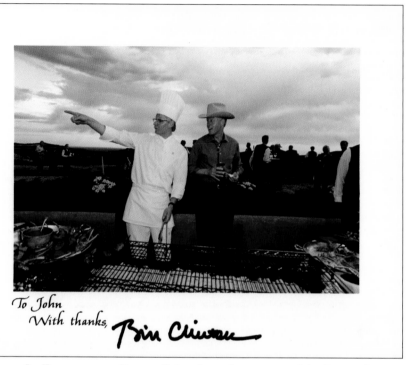

Dinner at Le Fort restaurant, Denver, Colorado on the occasion of the Denver Summit of the Eight, June 21, 1997. John Moeller and President Clinton. "No, Mr. President, we don't have elk—but we do have bison on that grill over there."

Shortly after that, the party was in full swing. Powerful world leaders casually moved around the terrace, talking and enjoying the buffet. About half an hour after I had to disappoint the President about elk, President Jacques Chirac of France approached my station. As with most of the participants, President Chirac had an interpreter with him. Out of habit, the French president spoke directly to his interpreter: "*Je veux un bien cuit.*" ("I'd like one well done.")

I replied to M. Chirac, "*Vous voulez un bien cuit?*" ("You'd like one well done?")

"*Oui, oui!*" he replied. ("Yes, yes!")

We continued to speak in French, and I offered, "Well, sir, these chops are double-cut, so how about if I split one in half?" (In English we call it a "butterfly cut"—but not in French.) "It will cook a bit faster that way."

"Ah, perfect!" he said, and we continued chatting for a few moments.

Walter noticed me conversing with President Chirac, and, not knowing exactly how good my French was, he grew a little nervous. The longer we talked, the more Walter worried that we might be having difficulty communicating, so he sent Patrice, a young French-born chef, over to help us out. Patrice appears in the photo of President Chirac and me, waiting to flip his lamb chop.

Dinner at Le Fort restaurant, Denver, Colorado on
the occasion of the Denver Summit of the Eight, June 21, 1997.
John Moeller and Patrice Olivon serving a grilled
chop to President Jacques Chirac of France.

Patrice discovered, of course, that there was no problem: that we were just passing the time with a little conversation while waiting for the meat to be well done. During the conversation, President Chirac looked at me and asked, "So, what part of France are you from?"

"Well, sir, I'm not French. I'm an American. I come from Lancaster, Pennsylvania."

"Oh, okay," he said. Then he added, "Your French is pretty good."

I had prided myself on my French pronunciation in the past, and people had occasionally been fooled by my authentic accent. I was especially comfortable speaking French when discussing food and cooking—my professional "home territory"—but this was the President of France! If he had started talking world politics or current events, I might have goofed up and revealed myself, but fortunately, we stayed in my conversational milieu, and he didn't guess that I was a French-speaking American.

What a privilege to have a casual chat with a world leader while grilling a lamb chop for him! I looked around and saw England's Prime Minister, Tony Blair, with his wife Cherie. Across the way, Boris Yeltsin was enjoying the buffet along with other fascinating public figures. It was awe inspiring, and I was a bit overwhelmed. I wanted to pinch myself.

John Moeller (foreground), with chefs serving dinner at Le Fort restaurant on the occasion of the Denver Summit of the Eight, Denver, Colorado, June 21, 1997.

Day after day, I showed my pass, entered the proper identification codes, and walked through the White House gates, but in all my years it never became completely routine. Whenever I approached the doors under the North Portico and gazed up at those majestic pillars, I found myself thinking, *Wow! I work at the White House!* I grew to appreciate the significance of our work. Being part of that "inner circle," I'd sometimes see a bit of rivalry among staff members—everyone was always trying to get closer to the president! The butlers and maids are naturally the closest—they're in the private residence most of the time, but we chefs get to know the first family fairly well. We have a lot of access, and the personal nature of preparing and serving food draws us pretty close.

As we prepared and served meals, the members of the first family would stop by the kitchen almost every day, to see what was going on, to ask a question, or to check on an upcoming event. The first lady might come to discuss a special guest coming to dinner in a day or two, and we'd talk about what to do: perhaps it would be good to prepare a nice salmon for Senator Stevens from Alaska; on the other hand, maybe it would be better not to serve salmon. Conversations like this helped me understand what a big role food can play in politics. It's amazing how much can be communicated by a meal, and how powerful an effect it can have. It brings people—even opponents—together in a more relaxed atmosphere.

If the conversation starts to get tense during a dinner meeting, the attendees can always back away from the tough issues and discuss the food and the way it's being presented. A tough-as-nails politician or billionaire will often become a different person when he sits down to a plate of good food and a glass of fine wine. Suddenly, the hard edge melts a little and everyone relaxes. Food and wine and good conversation have a way of calming the soul. Over the years, I've seen a warm, friendly meal tame that "inner tiger" on many occasions.

And this is what makes the work so worthwhile—the sheer pleasure of being able to work with quality ingredients and create a dining experience that brings joy to the guests. You can't ask for more than that!

SECURITY

G8 meetings usually have more than their share of demonstrations and protestors trying to make a point with these elite world leaders. While we were in Denver for the annual summit, we heard through the grapevine about an incident that started with a security breach. The delegates' spouses were scheduled for an excursion to Winter Park Resort one afternoon. Their itinerary called for them to ride Amtrak's "Ski Train" for the long trip out there. They got everyone on board and settled in for the ride. As the train was leaving Denver, a dozen protestors lined up along the track, bent over, and mooned the passengers — the G8 spouses in particular. While no real harm was done, the protestors shouldn't have been there — they shouldn't have known exactly when and where the G8 spouses would come through.

Security has always been primary where the White House and the president are concerned. During my time there, I watched security measures increase from a fairly routine set of rules to what they've become today. Almost everyone knows that security changed drastically after the 9/11 attacks, but even before that tragedy, other events had begun to impact our day-to-day lives.

We first started to feel the tightening security after the Alfred P. Murrah Federal Building was bombed in 1995. That incident set off a huge discussion in Washington about how to improve security at the White House. Some wanted to just close down Pennsylvania Avenue immediately. City and federal authorities had round after round of debates about the pros and cons. What would happen if someone actually pulled up in front of the White House and detonated a similar truck bomb? Experts said that a bomb like the one in Oklahoma City could do a lot of serious damage, but the main concern was the security of the president himself.

The Oklahoma City bombing happened less than a year after another highly publicized incident rattled nerves at the White House. In September 1994, a young man stole a small Cessna and managed to crash it into the White House at 2:00 a.m. The damage was minimal, and the pilot, who apparently died on impact, was the only casualty. I first heard of it on my car radio as I drove to work at six o'clock that morning. My reaction was "*Oh, my God! What's this all about?*"

Remember that this took place before Oklahoma City and seven years before 9/11. Our perspective was entirely different back then—we knew it was serious, but since the damage was minor, and the government downplayed it, the public moved on pretty quickly. When I arrived at the White House, I heard that the plane had smashed through the Jackson magnolia tree (planted by Andrew Jackson in 1835) and struck the White House wall a little below the State Dining Room. At that point, they didn't know whether it was an accident or a deliberate attack.

Once I got my morning work squared away, one of the officials walked me outside where investigators were taking measurements and shooting pictures. I stood there, looking at the aircraft, crumpled like an accordion, smashed up against the White House. It had barely missed a window in the presidential physician's office, and did some visible damage to the window and the wall.

We could see where the plane had approached from the south and made a gouge in the South Lawn grass. It crossed the circle drive, then crashed through the tree and crashed into the White House. There actually had been a ceremony scheduled that day on the south grounds. We speculated that the pilot had cut his engine and approached the South Lawn in the dark, but when he was low enough to see, there were the stages and grandstands set up for the next day's event.

It appeared that he steered toward the only area where there weren't any tables or chairs, and hit the grass hard enough to bounce—so he was airborne when he hit the White House. We could imagine the pilot's shock at seeing the cluttered South Lawn. He probably panicked when things weren't as he'd anticipated.

The first family wasn't even at home when the plane struck. They were staying across the street at Blair House because the White House air-conditioning system was being renovated. The pilot apparently acted alone, and it seemed to be more about suicide than an assassination attempt. The incident shook up the Secret Service and made a lot of people question White House security. A month later, there was another disturbing occurrence: a man with a semiautomatic rifle opened fire through the fence on the North Lawn. He shot thirty rounds before a couple of tourists tackled him. No one was hurt—President Clinton was actually upstairs watching a football game when the incident happened.

STATE DINNERS

State dinners provide an opportunity for the president to honor a world leader with a spectacular event that tells the visiting dignitary that he or she is important to the United States. At the same time, the president can showcase the White House and the power it represents. A state dinner leaves a deep and lasting impression.

It's easy to see the importance of a state dinner by the enormous amount of planning and preparation required. We usually received notice of a state dinner two months or so before the planned date. Sometimes we'd have three or four months' notice—especially for a really big event. As soon as the date is confirmed, all the department heads get busy. Of course the food is important, but that's only one piece of the puzzle. There's so much else to consider, from flower arrangements and decorations to security requirements and the final guest list.

Creating the guest list is one of the social secretary's biggest concerns. For example, if the president is giving the state dinner in honor of Japan's prime minister, she might want to include some prominent Japanese Americans on the invitation list. Depending on the guest of honor, the occasion, or the message the president wants to communicate, then she must figure out whom to invite and how to organize the best seating arrangements for all the guests.

If the dinner is to be served platter style, the social secretary must select the table hosts from among those guests who've been there before. Designating table hosts is a subtle process. They don't print the word "host" on the menu or the place card; rather, hosts are appointed quietly and instructed to lead the way for the other guests at their tables.

Being invited to the White House for any reason is a rare honor. To attend a state dinner leaves the average guest in awe of the pageantry, the celebrities, and the world leaders, and of being in the presence of the president and the first lady. I often wondered if most people even remembered the food at all!

Menu Planning

Many considerations go into selecting the food for a state dinner, but most important is pleasing the president and first lady as well as the visiting head of state and his or her spouse. We take good care of all the guests, but these four are our top priority. Making them happy begins with planning the menu. We already know what our first couple likes or dislikes, but we must learn about the guest of honor, so our social office contacts the Department of State, which contacts the embassy of the visiting dignitary to inquire into dietary preferences and restrictions. Whenever I planned a menu for a visiting dignitary, I usually didn't start writing things down till I had that information in hand. I didn't actually plan very many state dinners—Walter was in charge of that—but I planned many smaller dinners and working lunches, as well as a lot of meetings up at Camp David.

After we had the visitors' "do/don't do" list in hand, we could get serious about the menu. Here again, I found that we couldn't assume anything. One of the more memorable restriction lists I ever saw was for the Prime Minister of Italy. The notes read, "Does not like tomatoes, onions, or garlic." It was hard to believe he was really Italian, but we complied, and served him a very fine dinner with no onion, garlic, or tomato in it!

Knowing what to avoid, we could then begin to create a vision of which way to go. How should I develop the menu? I'd look at available seasonal items, because we liked to showcase regional foods from around the Washington area. Beyond that, we made sure to bring in seasonal items from elsewhere in the United States. I would draft two or three menus and submit them to the social secretary for consideration. The social secretary herself was often the first to make notes on proposed menus. She might make a suggestion: "Oh, I like this, but could we maybe do it this way?" Also, she sometimes had a directive from the first lady who perhaps wanted all seafood or a specific entrée: "Let's go with some wild king salmon."

We'd start with some proposals and then go back and forth with the social secretary and first lady to refine the choices. Through this dialogue, we'd finally come up with a menu that met the president's and first lady's approval. Often—especially for really important state dinners—we would do a tasting or two before settling on the final bill of fare. We'd prepare the menu for ten people, and serve a little dinner up on the second floor. This way, they could taste the items, see the actual presentation, and decide on any adjustments.

A state-dinner tasting always included the first lady and some of her key staff from the East Wing: her chief of staff, social secretary, and press secretary. Many times, the president sat in on the tasting, too. They would discuss the food and presentation, ask questions, and provide us feedback. Occasionally they asked for so many changes that a follow-up tasting was necessary. Once we'd finalized the menu, we sent it to the White House calligraphy department. The calligraphers handwrote all the menus and place cards for every guest at all official functions. Similarly, they handwrote all invitations to those on the guest list.

The social secretary continued to work with the floral department, too. They planned all the decorations and flower arrangements for the tables, and harmonized all the colors. They'd create a color theme and coordinate it with the selected china service, tablecloths, flowers, and napkins.

Food Preparation

We would plan to have all the needed food supplies on hand two days before an event. We wanted fresh ingredients, but also wanted enough time to make sure everything was up to standard. State dinners required a good two days' prep work as well. On the day of the function, we had to complete our prep and then execute the plan. Usually, we'd be having a fish course, a meat course, and a salad-cheese course, and then follow with a dessert. Our executive pastry chef took care of dessert, but the rest was up to us.

Sometimes we'd switch out the fish course for a soup or vegetable dish. We might do a yellow chanterelle mushroom soup or something equally exotic. We stayed away from meat soups, but prepared a lot of seafood. Lobster bisque was a favorite, and as with everything, we did our own interpretation. We made it with lots of lobster and interesting garnishes, so it was more distinctive than what you might find at a restaurant or hotel. We wanted all our guests to take a bite and say, "Wow—best I ever had!"

We often talked of the "direction" of our menu planning because that best described how we developed our plan. We worked "toward" an idea or two—a theme, an entrée—and built the details around it. That helped us avoid doing the same things over and over again. The "customers" were always the same, the president and the first lady, so we changed the menu.

Inspiration Is Everywhere

Where do the ideas come from? They're everywhere! I see something in a magazine or notice something on TV. I never copy the idea exactly. I might just like the overall appearance. Some little detail in a photo might catch my eye and trigger a new idea: an attractive way to carve a vegetable, or the way someone arranged julienne strips or placed something creative on top.

How can you keep things looking fresh and creative when you serve so many formal events? It's all about presentation. Some days, the ideas just seem to flow easily—other times, it's like having writer's block. One time I'll sit down and jot off a couple of menus in a few moments; the next time I find myself sitting there, thinking, *Hmm… what am I going to do with the lamb chop this time?*

I would get an idea and then start turning it over in my mind. *How can I make this a little different?* I imagine what the plate will look like. Sometimes I'd do a little demo for myself weeks ahead of time—sort of a one-man tasting. I'd try substituting different elements, and move things around the plate, or rework the vegetables. Our vegetable prep was more intense than cooking the meats. We would use multiple pieces of vegetable, color coordinating them and arranging them on the plate to please the eye and give a sense of style. It's not unlike a florist doing an arrangement. You can have the most beautiful flowers in the world, but how you put them in the vase makes all the difference in the world.

Place cards for formal dinners at the White House are prepared by the calligraphy department.

Staffers from the social secretary's office—well prepared with seating charts and guest lists—would lead each guest into the dining room and to his or her assigned seat. There's no chaotic search for seats—it all runs very smoothly.

Table setting at the State Dinner held at the White House to honor President Jiang Zemin, President of China, and Madame Wang Yeping. October 29, 1997.

Courtesy William J. Clinton Presidential Library.

Guests at the State Dinner in honor of His Excellency Jerry John Rawlings, President of the Republic of Ghana, and Nana Konadu Agyeman-Rawlings. February 24, 1999.

Courtesy William J. Clinton Presidential Library.

The Honorable
Leon E. Panetta

Entrance

Place cards for seating guests at the White House.

Throughout the event, the social-office staff kept alert and made it their business to know where each guest was. They listened to the arrival announcements, and kept tabs on who was still in the receiving line and who was just mingling in the Cross Hall, enjoying a cocktail and hors d'oeuvres before coming to the dining room. The butler staff manned the bars for the cocktail reception. They were all highly trained barmen, and the bars were well stocked. Guests could count on receiving virtually any beverage they might request.

Once everyone was seated in the State Dining Room, and the guests of honor were in place, the formal program would begin. Against the walls were what appeared to be decorative columns. Right before the first speech, they would part, revealing TV lights and cameras to record the event. From the first introductions, all platform speeches are recorded. The media can access them—C-SPAN often carries them live—and they create a historical record for the archives. The built-in camera and lighting systems helped avoid the chaos caused by media camera crews and boom microphones.

Usually, the visiting head of state made a short speech and offered a toast, followed by the president, who also spoke briefly and then toasted the guest of honor. When he finished and everyone sat down, it was time to begin serving. We listened at the door to hear our cue to send in the food. We didn't have the text of the president's speech to refer to, so we just opened the door a crack to hear. I tended to rely on the applause at the end of the speech to know when it was time to serve. A couple of times, however, I was fooled by spontaneous applause that erupted during the speech. I was at the door, heard clapping, and started to say, "Okay, guys, time to go!" Just one glance, though, and I saw that the president was still speaking. "Wait a minute—false alarm!" I put on the brakes and backed into the hall.

Once the speech was truly over, we sprang into action. The doors swung open and the servers entered the room with the first course. Our goal was always to get the entire meal done in an hour. With plated service, each butler carried two plates at a time, so we'd have fifteen butlers moving smoothly—but quickly—around the tables to get everyone served at almost the same time.

The social secretary had a backup plan to assure that there were no empty seats at a dinner. Alternates were always available to take the place of any invitee who couldn't make it. The invitations urged guests to advise the White House of any dietary concerns, such as food allergies, special diets, or conscience issues. Even if no one bothered to respond, we made sure to set up a few vegetarian plates just in case. And if, say, the social office told us there'd be two vegetarians in attendance, we always prepared four or five—who knew when a last-minute alternate might want vegetables only? We handled special requests with the same dedication to excellence as we did everything else. It was more than just avoiding an allergic-reaction incident; we wanted everyone to enjoy the White House experience, so we'd create a special plate without the ingredients that the guest was allergic to.

Daniel Shanks, one of the ushers during my tenure, was in charge of overseeing the butlers for big dining events. Part of his job was to make sure that special-request meals were served to the proper guests. He'd check the seating chart, determine which butler was serving that particular table, and remind the butler to serve the special meal to the guest who had requested it. I kept the special meals separate from the rest, so that when a butler came up out of that sea of servers and said, "I'm ready for that special meal," I could hand it directly to him and off he'd go.

After we'd covered the main courses, our pastry chef, Roland Mesnier, took over. He worked diligently with the social office and first lady to make sure that the meal ended with a flourish. His desserts were considered the *pièce de résistance*—the dramatic bit of culinary showmanship that left the guests in awe. Roland is a master of working with sugar and chocolate. Even for plated dinners, he usually served the desserts platter-style. He and his crew invested major time and effort decorating those dessert platters. As they saw these creations, you could hear guests throughout the dining room exclaim, "Ooh!" "Ah!" and "Wow!"

When a separate reception for dessert and coffee was being offered at the same time down on the Ground Level, we carefully coordinated the dessert reception with the timing of desserts being served in the State Dining Room. The dinner guests and the downstairs guests were merged on their way to the East Room on the State Level. The big mahogany doors of the East Room would open, and the crowd—some 200 by then—would flow inside to enjoy the evening's performance. The entertainment was always world-class, featuring nationally or internationally known artists of all kinds. Many times the evening concluded with dancing. The president and first lady might dance for a while before departing, but they always retired before the party wound down. They bade farewell to their guests and exited with the guests of honor, while others continued to enjoy the festivities.

It's funny—even after you've been a professional in a setting like this for some time, you can't help but have "stars in your eyes." Often, as we waited to begin service, I would open the door a crack. This allowed me to look around the room and see who was there. One evening we were waiting in the Green Room to serve one of our larger indoor state dinners in the East Room. I could see the president's table and the visiting Italian prime minister sitting there. I noticed a woman sitting at the president's table, and thought, *Oh, that's a good-looking woman sitting there with him!* As I studied her, I realized, *That's*

Easter Egg Roll

The White House Easter Egg Roll is held on the Monday after Easter and is a highlight of the annual calendar. Unlike diplomatic events, this is a fun occasion for families and children at the White House that follows a tradition started in 1878 by President Rutherford B. Hayes. Celebrities, performances, and activities are offered on the South Lawn. Attendance can top 30,000. Big-name actors and other public figures read stories and perform music, too. It's a huge event.

Easter at the White House.
Courtesy George Bush Presidential Library and Museum.

For years, the White House Historical Association, with the cooperation of the National Geographic Society, has published *The Living White House*, an overview of the presidents' home. First released in 1966, it's been updated several times, and in 1995, National Geographic released a TV movie, *Inside the White House*. The film crew came into the White House over a period of weeks, shooting footage of everything that goes on there. The groundbreaking film granted a behind-the-scenes look at the mansion and its operations.

I hadn't been working there long when they were shooting, but they did manage to capture me cooking and serving. There are always cameras around at the White House, so you just get used to having them pointed at you, but this was different—we were the subject of this film, which featured the people who take care of the president from day to day. Events that might not look very complicated to the public can require a surprising amount of work for their preparation and execution. The Easter Egg Roll is a good example.

The central Easter event is a little race for the children. Lanes are set up on the grass, with white cord to separate them. They look a little like miniature swim lanes. Each contestant rolls a colored egg, pushing it with a wooden spoon. The first one to the finish line wins. All day long they run heat after heat, giving thousands of children a chance to participate. Along with the eggs, the American Egg Board also sent hundreds of workers to help with the children's activities. They led in all kinds of games—including "egg toss."

The kitchen didn't produce much food that day, but we did boil a lot of eggs! Back in my time, the American Egg Board would send 10,000 raw eggs to the White House for us to prepare. The eggs would arrive on the Wednesday or Thursday before the event, and we'd start cooking them on Good Friday. To color the eggs, we'd boil them in a vinegar solution with food coloring added. We boiled eggs all day. Every table and counter in the kitchen would be covered with colored eggs, which had to cool before they could be put back in the crates and stacked in the refrigerator. That would be our Good Friday every year.

Our executive chef, Walter Scheib, established his own tradition: he took Easter weekend off every year to vacation with his kids—usually down in Florida. Being number two, I was left in charge of Easter-egg preparations every year, so when the press came calling on Good Friday to feature the great White House Egg Boil, there I'd be, cooking and coloring eggs. People found it interesting to see the preparations for the big Monday event. The major news networks would be there to tape segments about the background work.

One year, ABC-TV News came to do a live feed for *Good Morning America* when Charlie Gibson and Diane Sawyer were hosting the show. Since I was in charge, they hooked me up with a microphone while I worked. Suddenly, one of the directors said, "They're going to ask you some questions."

John Moeller prepares Easter eggs in the White House kitchen.

There was no TV in the room, so I wasn't conscious of the fact that while I worked and talked with them in the White House at 8:00 in the morning, everything was going out on live TV, all over the United States. I just showed them around and answered their questions about the eggs scattered all over the kitchen, unaware that millions of people were watching! Among many other questions, Charlie Gibson asked, "And can you actually eat these eggs?"

"Sure!" I responded. "Bring your saltshaker along if you want."

My answer cracked him up, and it provided a fun moment for their show. I was pretty relaxed—probably because I didn't know it was being broadcast live!

As the weather began to warm up, we'd start getting busier. May and June were demanding, building up to the annual Congressional Picnic in early June. The Congressional Picnic was a big event that emphasized the family focus of the White House. The Clintons liked to establish a theme for each one—one year it was Oktoberfest. We would set up two grill stations on the south grounds and serve from them and the main kitchen. Food was served as a picnic-style buffet; the guests served themselves, and we had servers on hand to assist as needed. We had special food, such as hot dogs, hamburgers, and ice cream for the kids, and we even had carnival rides set up on the south grounds for the families to enjoy. We served two or three thousand people for these events each year.

President Clinton thanking chefs after the
Congressional Picnic at the White House in 1998.

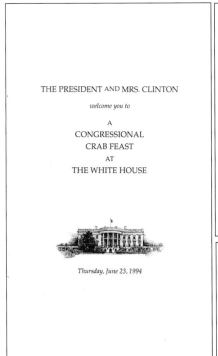

THE PRESIDENT AND MRS. CLINTON

welcome you to

A

CONGRESSIONAL
CRAB FEAST
AT
THE WHITE HOUSE

Thursday, June 23, 1994

PROGRAM

Living on the Wrong Side of Memphis
That's What I Like About You
If I Ain't Got You
The Song Remembers When
"X's & O's"
Down on My Knees
The Nightingale
She's in Love with the Boy
Walk Away Joe

TRISHA YEARWOOD

Trisha Yearwood
Vocals

Johnny Garcia
Guitar/Vocals

Jay Hagar
Bass

Ric McClure
Drums

Becky Priest
Keyboards

Heather Kolbrek
Fiddle

TRISHA YEARWOOD

Trisha Yearwood has had more success in three
years than many artists achieve in a lifetime. Ms.
Yearwood captures the essence of a song, from gutsy
blues tunes to heartfelt ballads. She has three hit
albums and her first album alone yielded four top
ten singles.
Trisha Yearwood grew up on a farm in Monti-
cello, Georgia and found her way to Nashville in
1985. Having worked her way up from a demo
singer for Nashville songwriters to the top of the
country charts, Trisha Yearwood has been singing
songs the way they ought to be sung for a long time.

MENU

Crisfield Crab Salad
Salisbury Marinated Tomatoes
with Corn Relish
Cabbage and Carrot Country Slaw
Herbed Potato Salad
Miss Minnie's Green Bean Salad
Hard Shell Crabs
Steamed in Beer and Old Bay
Rockfish with Lump Crab Stuffing
Eastern Shore BBQ Chicken
Corn on the Cob
Saturday Night's Baked Beans

Menu card and program for the
Congressional Crabfest at the
White House.
June 23, 1994.

July is one of the quieter months, and August is almost relaxed. The
president is often out for vacation while Congress is off for the month. Then,
September and October start to buzz with activity again. We're busy while
the president is in the house, but during November he would almost always
head out for international diplomatic trips. By then, of course, we were well
underway with the Christmas preparations. December arrives, and we're back
to Christmas season.

John Moeller serving President Clinton at a Christmas buffet.

To John Moeller
with appreciation,

White House resident staff with President Clinton and
Mrs. Hillary Rodham Clinton at Christmastime, 1997.

The White House staff is neutral—neither Democratic nor Republican. We were saddened to see the senior President Bush leave, but we were also happy serving the Clintons. Though we were just as brokenhearted to see them depart eight years later, we were looking forward to the next family, which would arrive that same day. We serve the presidency, not a particular individual or his party. Our job is to serve the President during his time in office, and to make the First Family as comfortable as possible during their time at the White House.

The Clintons bid farewell to the Bushes as the Clintons depart for Andrews Air Force Base during the Bush inaugural ceremony. January 20, 2001.
Courtesy William J. Clinton Presidential Library.

Menu for a Holiday Dinner at the White House on December 3, 2004

Holiday Dinner

Chanterelle Mushroom Soup
Goat Cheese Fritter
Patz & Hall Chardonnay "Hyde" 2002

Roast Tenderloin of Angus Beef
Black Truffle-scented Merlot Sauce
Sautéed Bulb Onion
Herb Potatoes
Green Beans and Artichokes
Paloma Merlot "Napa" 2001

Warm Tamale Salad
Avocado, Tomato, and Black Beans
Citrus Dressing

"Santa Claus is Coming to Town"
Lemon Mousse Tart · Raspberry Sorbet
Minted Champagne Sabayon Sauce
Mumm Napa Cuvée "Blanc de Noirs"

The White House
Friday, December 3, 2004

Menu card for a Holiday Dinner at the
White House on December 3, 2004.

Chanterelle Mushroom Soup,
Goat Cheese Fritter

*Roast Tenderloin of Angus Beef, Black Truffle–Scented Merlot Sauce,
Sautéed Bulb Onions, Herb Potatoes, Green Beans and Artichokes*

*Warm Tamale Salad; Avocado, Tomato,
and Black Beans; Citrus Dressing*

President George W. Bush and Mrs. Laura Bush stand in the Blue Room
of the White House for an official portrait. June 4, 2002.
Courtesy George W. Bush Presidential Library and Museum.

President George W. Bush and Mrs. Laura Welch Bush
(2001–2005)

Serving the Bushes

We wrapped up a particularly curious time that began with not knowing who had won the election and concluded with serving a new president and first lady who were part of a family we had already served.

President George H. W. Bush and his son, President George W. Bush, were two different men leading two different administrations, but the family connection made serving the George W. Bush White House unique. A photo that hung in the West Wing for a while during the son's term shows George W. Bush seated behind the desk in the Oval Office with his father standing, looking on. We referred to the photo as "The Two Presidents."

President George W. Bush sits at his desk in the Oval Office for the first time on Inaugural Day. He talks with his father, former President George H. W. Bush.

As with each Inauguration Day, the president and his family members are only in the White House for a short time in the afternoon—between the inauguration and all the balls and receptions of the evening. When George W. Bush became president, I was walking through the kitchenette area just off the third-floor Solarium and saw the President's sister, Dora, sitting and reading a newspaper.

"How ironic," I said. "I saw you leave here eight years ago, and now here you are, back again."

Dora recognized me, and said, "It's good to see you again."

President George W. Bush and Mrs. Laura Bush and Vice President Dick Cheney and Mrs. Lynn Cheney arrive onstage, January 19, 2005, during inaugural festivities on the Ellipse in Washington, D.C.

Courtesy George W. Bush Presidential Library and Museum.

President George W. Bush and
Mrs. Laura Bush dance at an inaugural ball,
January 20, 2001, in Washington D.C.
Courtesy George W. Bush Presidential Library and Museum.

President George W. Bush and Mrs. Laura Bush
dance together during the Commander in Chief Ball,
January 20, 2005, at the National Building Museum in
Washington, D.C.
Courtesy George W. Bush Presidential Library and Museum.

The first months of the new administration—through spring and early summer—found us serving a number of events, but not big, elaborate functions. The Clintons had expanded state dinners beyond the confines of the State Dining Room, with its 130 to 140 capacity, and they seemed to get bigger throughout his presidency—with the 950-guest NATO celebration at its peak. The Bushes, too, kept the White House busy with official and social events, and mostly they were of a size that could be accommodated back in the State Dining Room once again. Their first State Dinner was held on September 5, 2001 in honor of the President of Mexico, Vicente Fox and First Lady Marta Sahagún.

Summer came to a close following the usual pattern, and we began our annual Christmas preparations in early September, but in the second week, "September 11" Took on a whole new significance.

That day changed everything at the White House forever.

SEPTEMBER 11

Everyone is painfully aware of the events of September 11, 2001, but we had a different perspective from inside the White House. The annual Congressional Picnic, which is a huge party, was scheduled for that evening. We were preparing for more than 2,000 people—members of Congress and their guests—to begin arriving around 5:00 p.m. for a Texas-style barbeque. In the kitchen, we were in full production mode when someone came and announced, "Hey, it looks like a plane just crashed into the World Trade Center."

My first thought was that there might have been an accident with small aircraft like the one that had crashed into the White House years earlier. We were too busy preparing for the barbeque to spend much time thinking about it. I was helping with the main event, and I was also on "do Family" That day. As I got ready to prepare lunch for Mrs. Bush, I took a moment to step away from what I was doing and went to catch a peek at the little TV set near the storeroom. On the screen was a burning skyscraper (the North Tower), and as I watched, I saw what appeared to be a plane crashing into the building. I was confused. *How can they get a picture of the building burning before the plane hit it?* One of the guys watching the TV said, "I think that's another plane!"

As it turned out, I had walked up to the TV just as the second plane hit the South Tower. We were all disoriented—standing there trying to figure out what the hell was going on in New York. As we puzzled over it, the chief usher, Gary Walters, walked up behind me. "There's no party tonight," he said. "This looks like a terrorist attack. Let's get all this food put away and the kitchen area secured. Then we'll get the temporary employees out of the building. Only White House pass holders will stay."

With a new task at hand, we shook off what we'd heard so far and got back to the kitchen to break things down. We turned off ovens and equipment and packed up product for refrigeration. We had staffed up for the big event, and had fifteen temporary chefs working with us in the kitchen and out on the south grounds. When the cancellation notice came, Walter Scheib was outside, directing the operation. He and his crew were arranging grills and equipment, and setting up tables and chairs, so I made sure the kitchen crew got things put away, while I continued to prepare Mrs. Bush's lunch. The President wasn't in the house—he was at an event down in Florida, and was scheduled to arrive home in time for the Congressional Picnic, so I had only Mrs. Bush for family lunch. As I finished the lunch preparations, I didn't realize that the First Lady had actually been up on Capitol Hill when the events of 9/11 had begun to unfold.

President George W. Bush watches television coverage of the terrorist attacks on the World Trade Center, September 11, 2001, from his office on Air Force One.

Courtesy George W. Bush Presidential Library and Museum.

The phone rang. I picked it up, and Brian Williams was on the line. An army food-service specialist who often helped us with special events, he was supposed to bring an army field kitchen from Fort McNair to the White House for our barbeque. "What the heck is going on? I'm having a hard time getting this field kitchen over there."

Brian was stuck in traffic a block away, and didn't have his radio on, so he had no idea what was happening. He was getting anxious. "There's a lot of traffic out here—and people all over the place. It makes me nervous because I'm carrying a truck full of volatile fuel."

Rather than liquid propane, the field-kitchen trucks used a type of jet fuel, which allowed military units to transport and manage fewer types of fuel. You could cook with it or power a helicopter. I explained to Brian what we knew about New York and told him, "We just got word that the party is canceled. You might as well just turn around and head back to McNair. We can talk later."

Before I could hang up the phone, Walter burst into the kitchen, breathless. "The Pentagon just got hit!" he said. "We could be next—everybody out of here!"

I didn't even tell Brian goodbye. I just set the phone down and said, "The Pentagon got hit? What the hell is going on?"

I looked at the stoves. We'd been breaking things down for half an hour since seeing the second plane hit the World Trade Center on TV. I turned off the burner under Mrs. Bush's minestrone and looked around the kitchen. It was like a bad dream: *Is this really happening? Are we really evacuating the White House?*

The Pentagon is situated across the Potomac, no more than a mile away. You can actually see the building itself from up in the Solarium, but the view is obstructed down on the grounds. Up on the south grounds, Walter and his crew were still breaking down the outdoor setup when Flight 77 smashed into the western wall of the Pentagon. They heard the explosion and saw the plume of black smoke towering into the sky to the south, and made a dash for the White House.

Everywhere you looked, you could see people exiting the White House. It was like a well-organized fire drill—no panic, no screaming, and no running for the doors. We exited through the maze of hallways and doors under the North Portico. This area by the storerooms and walk-in coolers was our "home turf." Staff members flowed through this passage constantly on their way to either of the White House wings. A Secret Service agent was always stationed in this hallway, outside my kitchen door. He monitored hallway traffic, making sure everyone coming through had the proper pass and clearance. When I finally stepped from the kitchen, I saw the agent standing there, watching us leave. His expression wasn't the usual stoic look you expect to see on an agent's face. He had a spooked look in his eyes.

I'll never forget that look—and it shook me. *These guys never show emotion! What has he been listening to in his earpiece?* I couldn't help but wonder what horrible information he might have access to that we knew nothing about. That subtle look of horror in his eyes haunted me, as I made for the exit. We

Even though it was only lunchtime, we decided to drive over to the school and pick up our boys. Something in us just wanted to gather our sons and be together as a family. Our older son, Alexander, was in third grade at the same school where Zachary was going to kindergarten. At the school, we found a lot of parents with the same idea. The school office staff had worked out a system with walkie-talkies: as each child's parents came to the office, they'd notify the principal, who was out on the playground with the children. When it was our turn, they called, "The Moeller family is here for Zachary and Alexander. Bring them on in."

I went outside to look for the boys, and talked with the principal for a few moments. Of course, he already knew what I did for a living, so he asked me some questions about my morning. As we talked, fighter jets screamed through the air overhead, patrolling the skies around our nation's capital. It was sobering. Americans have gotten used to life without really seeing our military actively guarding us on a daily basis. It was beginning to sink in that we were living through something grave. We loaded into the car and headed back home, wondering what to do about the birthday party we had planned for Zachary that evening. Originally, I wasn't even going to be there because of the Congressional Picnic scheduled for that night. Nonetheless, my wife had planned to have a few of Zach's friends come over with their parents. Several parents called to see if we were going to continue with our plans.

"Well, if you still want to come, we'll have something," we responded. In the end we had seven families show up with their kids. Zachary was only five, and had no idea what was going on across the country. Why should he miss his birthday? I went to the supermarket and picked up some hamburger. My plan was to do something easy—burgers-on-the-grill stuff. There were already beers in the fridge, so we sat around my family room with a half-dozen couples, looking at the TV and digesting the day's events. By suppertime we had a lot more information, and processing all of that together with a group of friends turned out to be therapeutic for us. The kids were outside, playing and having a good time; the parents were inside, getting through a very tough time together.

I learned later that when President Bush learned about the attacks, he became anxious to wrap up his visit with the schoolchildren in Florida and get back to the White House. That turned out to be a challenge. First, his security people had to determine whether it was safe for him to return, and after they'd made that decision, there was another complication: there was no place for Marine One, the big Sikorsky helicopter, to land. Marine One generally lands on the South Lawn, but the Congressional Picnic setup prevented that. The President had left that morning by limousine, and Marine One had picked him up near the Lincoln Memorial Reflecting Pool on the mall. They wanted to bring him directly back to the White House grounds, but first they had to clear a place for the helicopter. If you look at news footage of the President's return to the White House that day, you'll not only see the helicopter on the grounds, but you can also see tables and chairs in disarray, shoved aside to make way for a helicopter landing.

Later in the evening, I managed to get Walter on the phone. He was able to get through to the chief usher and managed to get back into the White House. They were monitoring the situation at the White House and would be able to give us further instructions as events continued to develop. Walter told me that he and a few others were working in the kitchen to turn some of that extra food we'd prepped into a big buffet for Secret Service and other staff who were there that night. He indicated that we'd pull things together when I came in the next morning. I told him, "I'll have to ride the Metro in, because my car is still down there."

I didn't know what driving in DC would be like the next day, and I didn't want my wife to have to deal with it, so I just took the 5:30 a.m. train. When I arrived, we had to figure out what to do with our surplus of food. Not only had we canceled the Congressional Picnic, but everything else was also postponed or canceled. We arranged for a truck to pick up a load of food and take it out to some of the military units in the DC area. I went along to help deliver to Fort McNair and Fort Myer. We spent the whole morning distributing food, and I didn't get back to the White House till midday.

In the afternoon, we had to look at our schedules and work assignments. Naturally, the entire White House social calendar was already headed for the paper shredder, but even though everything was canceled, that didn't mean we'd be without work. For the next two months, the President and First Lady would entertain a constant stream of high-profile heads of state—but these wouldn't be big parties and state dinners. Several times a week, we prepared

The American flag flies at half-mast over the White House at sunrise, September 14, 2001, as counter assault team (CAT) members are posted on the roof.

Courtesy George W. Bush Presidential Library and Museum.

President George W. Bush and Vice President Dick Cheney are joined by White House staff members, September 18, 2001, as they observe a moment of silence on the White House South Lawn.

Courtesy George W. Bush Presidential Library and Museum.

food for working lunches and dinner meetings. One was off site: we went to Camp David to take care of a dinner meeting with Prime Minister Tony Blair of England. The President was strengthening relationships, building a military coalition. No parties, no receptions, just serious business meetings—servicing these and taking care of the First Family consumed our days.

After a couple of months of this new, somewhat grim, work environment, I had a casual conversation with one of the Secret Service agents who served in the PPD, the Presidential Protection Division. Over the years, I got to know several of these dedicated agents, and came to realize that their jobs gave them access to a lot of information not available to the rest of us. As on every day during that period, we discussed the topics on everyone's mind: the terrorist attacks, continuing threats, and security. He mentioned something that I found very disturbing: "There's a lot of evidence to show that we might have been the intended target of the plane that hit the Pentagon. When you look at the plane's final course, it headed toward the Pentagon, then veered away, and then circled back around toward the Pentagon. It didn't hit the wall like the ones that hit the Twin Towers. It actually hit the ground first and skidded across the macadam before going through the wall at ground level."

He believed the evidence showed that the hijackers were actually looking for the White House, but that it was much more difficult to see from the sky. It's hard to pick it out from among all the government buildings in that area. Our minds had been saturated with images of the Twin Towers' destruction. The media kept replaying the footage—the pictures were burned into our minds. I started thinking about the "what-ifs." I mentally pictured the explosions and the extent of the damage to the Twin Towers. Then I imagined what an explosion that size would do to the White House. It seemed clear that a similar plane crash would have consumed the entire building, and we would all have been wiped out.

The administration brought in grief counselors to talk to us immediately after 9/11. I don't remember thinking about it all the time, but weeks after the events, I suddenly found myself turning things over in my mind—dwelling on the reports and rumors I'd heard. It was hard not to be consumed with it all.

Immediately after 9/11, people from the National Park Service started coming through the kitchen to use our service elevator to access the third floor. They were bringing potted trees upstairs. We found out that they were taking them up to the White House roof where they built a miniature forest to provide a little camouflage that would make it harder to spot the White House from the air. Those trees stayed up there till December.

The White House curators provided another odd twist in the daily routine. They brought in recording equipment to tape my recollection about 9/11. They wanted to hear my version of what had happened around me. They recorded and transcribed it, word for word, for the historical record, and then offered me a copy of the transcript, which I keep filed away.

As the weeks went by, we continued to plan for Christmas, despite the fact that the fall social calendar had been completely abandoned. We planned the menus, got them approved by the First Lady and the social secretary; Roland did long-range prep work for cookies and cakes, and decorations and flowers were designed.

But, it was like working in a dream—we were just trying to maintain some kind of routine. Like all Americans, we were trying to absorb what had happened and adjust to some kind of new reality that we still did not understand.

At Thanksgiving time, First Lady Laura Bush informed the entire White House staff: "I know it's only been a few weeks, but we have to push ourselves to move on—if only a little. We'll never forget what happened, but we have to start entertaining again."

From that point, our calendar started to fill up once more. It built gradually at first, and by Christmastime, we were back to the business of hosting guests at the White House once again.

The Post-9/11 White House

B ut it was never truly "business as usual" again. The White House was not the same jolly place I had joined nearly ten years earlier. We couldn't shake the sense that we were "Target number one—the next Ground Zero." After Christmas and New Year's, it remained obvious that no one was the same after the 9/11 tragedy. I could see it in the eyes of the President and the First Lady, whom it affected as profoundly as it had all other Americans. The presidency aside, they were both human beings.

And, this unease was fueled by the new security consciousness. The Secret Service and the FBI met with us to discuss all our procedures. They wanted to know how we did everything. Where did we get food? Who had knowledge and access? They said they had information leading them to believe that our enemies planned an attempt to deliver something through our food network. "We all have to be vigilant," They told us. "Look at everything. Watch for vulnerabilities."

In response, we changed a number of our procedures.

We saw strange sights all the time. One day after the attacks, I was walking down East Executive Boulevard toward my car and noticed a plain white van sitting there with its engine running. I paid little attention until I noticed it again the next day… and the day after that… and the day after that. It was there every day. Near the back of the van, I saw what appeared to be a little smokestack. When I walked by, I heard a "whoosh" That sounded like air flowing through it. After a month, I noticed that a heavy-duty power cord had been run out to the van, and the engine was no longer idling. Eventually, I learned that the van was full of equipment that constantly sampled the air near the White House to test for contaminants. That van sat there for at least two years.

I don't know how many small planes drifted into secure airspace near the White House during the years before 9/11, but afterward, an errant Cessna could set off total panic. The first time it happened, I was on duty one Sunday night when the President was in the residence by himself. It was quiet, and just one butler, Ramsey, and I were serving the President's dinner. He almost always dined at 7:00 when he was alone. I took dinner up to the butler for service. After cleaning the the upstairs kitchen I loaded my cart and, as I waited at the elevator door to head back down, I noticed the butler rinsing some plates down in the kitchen. The running water kept him from hearing the President, who called out from the dining room, "Ramsey! There's an airplane heading our way! Get down to the bomb shelter!"

What had the President just said? I couldn't see him from the elevator entry, but his voice was coming from the main hallway near the dining room. Ramsey shut off the water and stuck his head around the corner, so he could see me in the alcove by the elevator. "Was that the President?"

"Yeah, I think so."

"What did he say?"

"If I heard him right," I replied, "he said there's an aircraft heading our way, and we need to get down to the bomb shelter."

Ramsey looked at me. "Well, what do you think we should do?"

"I don't know about you, but I'm going to the bomb shelter."

Just then, the elevator doors slid open and we both got in. I reached for the "B" button to go to the basement, but as we started to descend, I remembered: "Hey! The pot washer's in the kitchen!" So I punched the "G" for Ground Floor where the main kitchen is located. When the doors opened, I yelled, "Clarence!"

"What?"

"Get over here!"

"What's going on?" he asked.

"Just get over here and get in the elevator!"

He headed our direction and asked again, "What's going on?"

I told him what we'd heard, and said, "Come on — we're going to the bomb shelter."

There was hardly anyone in the whole building, and stopping for Clarence had cost us a few minutes, so by the time the doors opened in the basement we saw no one. We wasted no time heading down the hall toward the heavy blast doors that marked the bomb-shelter entrance. The second I stepped off the elevator, I could hear the beep, beep, beep of the automatic doors as they were shutting. My heart skipped a beat—"We're not going to make it!"

The Secret Service agents had gotten the President inside and were sealing the shelter. You know, God loves us all, but the Secret Service has one primary job: to secure the president. The three of us just looked at each other, and I said, "Now what are we going to do?"

The only thing I could think of was to get out of there: "I don't know—let's go back upstairs and leave the White House."

We hurried back up to the ground floor and cut through the kitchen toward the exit under the North Portico—the area where a Secret Service agent always stands watch. We tried the doors, only to find them locked, and three agents were there, instead of the usual one.

"Nobody in—nobody out," said one of them.

"What do you mean?" I was incredulous.

"It's a lockdown," he said without emotion. "Nobody in—nobody out."

"Come on, guys," I coaxed. "We just want to leave. Can't you let us out?"

"Nobody in—nobody out."

"Come on! It's just us!" I felt a little panic rising in my throat. "Don't you take some kind of oath to protect us? Can't you just open the door and let us leave?"

Expressionless, he repeated, "Nobody in—nobody out. It's a lockdown."

The weirdest fifteen minutes of my life started at that moment. I was standing there in a dreamlike state. I looked around at this familiar environment, thinking, *Is this it—is this the end?* A bizarre feeling of utter helplessness overwhelmed me. I felt totally exposed, as I stood there with my butler and pot washer. Nothing seemed real, as I wondered if I was about to be vaporized at any moment. Suddenly, I felt anger, and thought, *Is this even worth it? Do I really want to live my life like this?* It's odd what crosses your mind during a moment of extreme crisis—when you justifiably wonder, *Am I going to die now?*

After the crisis passed, those feelings began to die down, but they'd still sneak up on me from time to time. They don't necessarily consume you, but they nibble at your mind continually. How do you ignore the fact that someone out there is probably targeting you because of where you work? That wasn't the last time we found ourselves hurrying to the shelter. Small planes wander too close and penetrate restricted airspace fairly often. It began to feel as if it only happened when I was on duty. It seemed I'd almost always be up on the second level, serving the family, when we got the word, and then it was drop everything and down to the bomb shelter we'd go.

Several times, I stepped out of the elevator and into the shelter just ahead of the closing blast doors. They'd seal, and we'd be standing there with other staff members, listening to the silence. The memory of standing face-to-face with the President and the First Lady in a bomb shelter will never leave me. Behind concrete and steel with the leader of the free world, we all wondered what might be going on up above. I found myself thinking philosophically: *What have I done with my life? What am I all about?* The big questions that are usually buried in our day-to-day routines surface in the midst of events like that.

Mrs. Reagan and the Dover Sole

During those days, former First Lady Nancy Reagan was in town for a visit. She enjoyed an open invitation to stay at the White House whenever she was in the DC area. She stayed for two days. The President and the First Lady were there to entertain her the first day, but they had to leave town the second day. Mrs. Reagan's visit coincided with one of those times when I had all-day family duty. I was responsible for breakfast, lunch, and dinner, and I really wanted to do something special for her to make her stay with us comfortable and memorable.

Wouldn't you know it—a stray airplane popped up on the radar that day, and the Secret Service had to get her out of the second floor and help her down to the shelter. We all felt bad for her, an eighty-one-year-old woman having her pleasant visit interrupted for a trip to the bomb shelter. We assumed it must have been a harrowing experience for her—but it certainly made for a memorable stay at the White House, I'm sure.

Mrs. Reagan's visit had turned out to be more memorable than I'd hoped—and for all the wrong reasons! But before our misguided-airplane incident, I recognized an opportunity to show her the respect and kindness due to her. When the butler brought down Mrs. Reagan's breakfast menu card, it struck me that I could give her some extra attention, since the First Family was away. I suggested to the butler, "Why don't you ask Mrs. Reagan what she's in the mood for tonight? Tell her she can have anything she would like."

The butler took breakfast up and returned to tell me, "Mrs. Reagan said she loves Dover sole. That would be perfect." She had also given the butler some suggestions for garnishes and side dishes.

"No problem," I said confidently. "I'll call my local seafood guys."

Did I say "no problem"? Wouldn't you know it—I couldn't find a single piece of fresh Dover sole anywhere in the DC area. It was frozen or nothing at all. I thought, *There's no way I can serve frozen fish to the former First Lady of the United States!* But I had made a promise, and now I was on a quest. I called one of my fish guys up in the Boston area. I had some good connections with the seafood industry in New England.

"Hey," I said, "do you have any Dover sole?"

"We get fresh Dover sole in here every day!"

"Okay, I just need one fish."

"Hmm…what time is it?" My contact looked at the clock and saw that it was 9:30 in the morning. "I've got a truck going over to Boston Logan Airport in a little while, and I'm sure I can have it down to you within the next two hours."

I talked to a couple of guys—including a Secret Service agent—and they drove over to Reagan National Airport to meet the shuttle flight from Boston. They picked up the box and had it on my kitchen counter by 1:30 that afternoon. Now that I had a Dover sole to work with, I could provide the former First Lady with exactly what she had requested for that evening. I was glad to have all the White House resources at my disposal that day, and considering Mrs. Reagan's traumatic midday interruption, I was especially happy that I didn't have to resort to frozen fish for her dinner.

CONTINUING TO SERVE THE BUSHES

During the George W. Bush administration, it was always a pleasure to see former President George H. W. Bush and Barbara Bush again. When they were in the White House from time to time, they made a point to come by the kitchen just to say hello to everyone and ask how we were doing. We had all felt close to them during their term in office, and we grew even closer as we saw them during their son's presidency.

Our cooking emphasized regional and seasonal ingredients, and I took advantage of my connections up in Lancaster on several occasions. Rural Pennsylvania produces some remarkable vegetables—some of the best sweet corn in the world is grown there, and the tomatoes are outstanding. Whenever I was in the area, I shopped for local produce and brought it back with me. I enjoyed telling the First Lady about the vegetables we served, proud that they came from the farms around my boyhood home. Even after I moved to Maryland, I always kept a good-sized garden at home. I loved bringing in my own produce and describing my organic growing methods for the First Lady. And Mrs. Bush appreciated it—especially my dedication to pure organic gardening.

President Bush's birthday is July 6, so we always celebrated it as part of our Fourth-of-July festivities. It was a natural time to break out the barbeque and party out on the South Lawn. One year I was searching for some fresh corn for the President's birthday. What's a July Fourth cookout without corn on the cob? I knew my dad was driving down to visit my sister for the weekend, so I called him and asked if he could help. Dad tracked down a couple of crates of sweet corn picked that very morning by a farmer up in the Lancaster area.

He picked it up in the morning as he was leaving to drive down to DC. I arranged to meet him at a spot near the Beltway. We transferred the corn from his car to my van, and I brought it back to the White House. I had it boiling by 5:00 p.m., and by six o'clock, the President and his guests were enjoying it down on the south grounds. Everyone commented on how great it was—and there wasn't one ear left at the end of the dinner!

It's all about striving to serve the best food—and doing whatever it takes to find the best ingredients and prepare it with excellence. I got lucky that weekend, because my dad was already heading down from Lancaster, but I'd have found another way if he hadn't been available.

If you don't start with great products to work with, you can't expect to serve great food. The better your ingredients, the more likely you'll end up with a nice dish to serve. I had favorite suppliers, but I never bought everything from only one place. I wouldn't settle for "good enough," and if I found something not quite up to par, I'd just keep going till I found what I was looking for.

Sometimes it is a pain to always be on the lookout for products that are up to my standards, but the results are totally worth it!

A Pretzel Twist

When the Clintons were in the White House, the First Lady asked us to find some good, healthy foods and beverages to keep in the upstairs kitchen for them to snack on between meals. We stocked the fridge and pantry up there with bottled water and a variety of items they could just grab whenever they felt like it.

Back in Lancaster, we had a favorite pretzel made by a local, family-owned bakery. I brought some back with me whenever I went home. They were just another part of our snack inventory until suddenly we couldn't keep them in stock. It turned out that Chelsea had discovered them and absolutely loved them. The kitchen phone rang one day, and when I answered it, the ushers' office asked, "Who's bringing in those pretzels?"

"That would be me," I answered.

"Well," he continued, "the First Lady wants to know the name and address of the pretzel maker." I gave him the information and didn't give it another thought.

A month later, I went up to Lancaster and, as was usual now, stopped by the bakery. Just inside the door was a bulletin board on which they posted notes of appreciation and testimonials from all over the country. They filled pretzel orders nationwide, and people took time to write, "You've got a great product," or "Best pretzel I've ever eaten." You'd see notes from Alabama, Washington State, and more. As I glanced at the board, the White House emblem caught my eye. There was a letter from First Lady Hillary Rodham

Clinton on White House stationery: "It's so nice to have a good, healthy snack food that tastes great."

I caught the attention of Carol, one of the owners, and said, "Oh, I see she sent a letter."

Carol beamed. "Yeah! You know, it's funny how people come in here all the time and look over the board. They're so used to seeing notes from John or Jane Doe out in Iowa or Kansas that they hardly give it a thought. But they do a double take when they notice the White House letter. They're so impressed to see a note like that in our little shop."

The pretzels had been such a hit that I continued to keep the supply coming even after we changed bosses. President George W. Bush liked them, too. One Sunday evening in January 2002, the President was up in the residence by himself, watching a football game. He was snacking, and somehow managed to choke on a piece of pretzel that lodged in his throat. It turns out that it was serious—the President actually fainted momentarily and fell from the couch. He suffered a bruise and a scrape on his face when he hit the floor. He had to be checked out by the White House physician the next day. The story hit the media, of course, because the White House had to explain the obvious facial injuries. I felt especially bad about the whole thing because I had supplied the pretzels—and from my own hometown! The next time I was up there—a month later—I stopped into the bakery again. The owner gave me a look, and just said, "Was it?"

I nodded. "Yeah, it was."

We both felt the need for discretion that day. It was nice for them to have it known that their product was a favorite at the White House, but they obviously didn't want to become famous for having produced the pretzel that almost took out the President of the United States!

An incident like this helps you appreciate how complicated the work is for the agents of the President's Protection Detail. There was always an agent right there outside the door. The first family can summon immediate help with one of the panic buttons located in the apartment, but if the president or a family member is alone and can't reach a panic button—you never know what could happen.

As we interacted within that inner circle around the First Family, it was easy to forget that they were getting to know us a little bit, too. The longer I served them and chatted casually with them from time to time, the more they learned about me. The President could show up in the kitchen any time—maybe to grab a bottle of water or some ice to put on his knees after a workout. We might exchange a few words—usually about what was on the menu that night, but never about policy or politics. The residence was a politics-free zone, as far as staff was concerned.

One day during his 2004 reelection campaign, President Bush happened to be eating by himself again, so there were only a couple of us taking care of him, and it was pretty quiet around the kitchen. I was finishing up my duties when he stepped into the kitchen and said, "Hey."

"Hey, Mr. President," I responded. "I see that you were up in my neck of the woods yesterday."

He had been in Reading, Pennsylvania, and had swung down through Lancaster for a personal appearance. He paused a moment, then said, "Oh! You're from Lancaster?"

"Yeah, that's my hometown."

"Oh, boy, I love that place."

"Really?"

"I have great support from the folks up there. I enjoyed seeing the people out on the streets there. This was my first time visiting Lancaster, and I really, really loved it!"

We talked about Lancaster for a few minutes. He returned to my city a couple more times during that campaign, and always enjoyed consistent support from the community. In 2011, the Lancaster Chamber of Commerce invited him back to speak for a dinner that was attended by a capacity crowd of over 2,500 people.

My father worked as an air traffic controller and manager at Lancaster County Airport. He really enjoyed those visits when Air Force One came into his airport. On one campaign stop, they held the event right at the airport. All the local politicians were out in full colors, and as airport manager, Dad was able to get tickets for my mom and him to get up close. As the President and Mrs. Bush worked the crowd, Mom called out to them when they got close enough, "Mrs. Bush?"

Laura Bush heard her and turned. "Yes?"

"Oh, I just wanted to introduce myself," said my mom. "My son, John Moeller, is one of your chefs down at the White House."

"Oh, we know John!"

The President's twin daughters, Barbara and Jenna, were there, too. "Oh, yeah, we know John, and we love the great produce he brings us from Lancaster!"

Once again, the First Lady showed her graciousness; she had taken a moment out of her busy schedule to acknowledge my mom. It was a very special moment for her.

Space Shuttle Columbia

It was a fine Saturday morning in February 2003. I had a light weekend, because President and Mrs. Bush were spending the weekend at Camp David. Enjoying a little "family time," I was at my son's basketball game in Rockville, watching a pack of second-graders running up and down the court. I was just being a dad watching a ballgame with other parents. I had carpooled with a neighborhood mom and her son, and we were having a great time.

My cell phone rang. It was Skip, the usher on duty at the White House that weekend. He said, "The President's coming back at noon — and he wants lunch. There'll be six to eight people."

With almost no information, I turned to my neighbor and said, "Maria, I've got to leave. Something has happened, and I've been ordered to get down to work ASAP."

"I'm ready to leave, too," she answered.

It was around 9:30 a.m., and the ballgame was almost over anyway, so we went down to the sidelines and picked up our sons to head for home. The whole time my mind was racing, wondering what was going on. We made our way to the car, and my radio was, as usual, tuned to the local news. Right away, we heard that the space shuttle *Columbia* had exploded on reentry, and the President had decided to leave Camp David and return to the White House immediately.

Sizing up the situation, I started a mental inventory of what was on hand in the White House kitchen. We didn't keep excess food on hand — even less for a weekend when the First Couple were at Camp David. We would have a few things to fix for them when they returned Sunday evening, but there wouldn't be much. As I thought about what was in the refrigerators, I turned over possibilities in my mind.

I called the White House engineering department, knowing I could count on them because they had people there 24/7. They constantly monitor the White House, and are always ready to take care of anything that might need attention. When the engineer on duty answered, I said, "I need you to go up to the kitchen. Put a big pot of water on to boil — I don't know what I'm going to do with it, but just get it started. Turn on the ovens to three-fifty, start the grills, get out a cutting board, and lay out my knives. Then go in the fridge, bring out whatever vegetables you see, and put them on the table." I wanted the grill hot so I could quickly mark some meat if I needed to.

I was still trying to think of what I could throw together quickly. I knew I had some chicken stock that I'd just made the day before, so I asked him to pull that out of the fridge, too. "I think I can make a quick soup out of that."

It took a little time to drop off our friends at home, get back to my house, and get ready to go. By the time I got my son in the house, grabbed my White House keys and ID, and started driving, it was 10:20 a.m. It normally took thirty-five minutes to drive to the White House—in light traffic. I careened down 270 and the Clara Barton Parkway to Canal Road—the fastest way I knew—and arrived at 11:00. I paused for a breath, and then looked over my ingredients. After a few minutes' thought, I finally came up with an idea for a lime tortilla soup. I had what I needed to make quesadillas, and I put together a little salad with avocados.

The President landed at 11:30, and we had lunch before them by noon. I could hardly believe I pulled it off—wasn't even sure how it all happened. Even though I had to improvise the menu and pull the meal together so fast, the result still had to be first class! This was really an extraordinary situation. "Emergency" meals very rarely happened at the White House. We usually had plenty of notice, but once in a while "things happen."

After lunch, I discovered that not only would I need to take care of the President and Mrs. Bush, but that they had also decided to invite some guests for dinner. Suddenly, I had to prepare a dinner for fourteen in just a few hours. Back to the trusty engineers: "Hey, guys, we have to go to the market and buy some groceries."

There was no way I had enough food on hand to serve that many people, so I worked up a menu, made a shopping list, and off we went. We brought back the ingredients and I started cooking—then realized the pastry department wasn't on hand. I hardly ever made desserts at the White House—after all, we had one of the finest pastry chefs anywhere for that purpose. If we needed a little something on the weekends, he'd simply prepare it and leave it for us to serve.

I thought, *Well, let me see what I can do.* One of my reliable favorites came to mind: a warm, flourless chocolate torte. I dug out the recipe and prepared a dessert to go along with dinner. No big deal—just something one might have to do from time to time. Dinner went off without a hitch. Everyone had a great time and enjoyed the food, and when the butlers served the dessert, the diners said, "Be sure to say thanks to the pastry department for this great torte!"

The butlers admitted, "Actually, that dessert came from John—he's the only one here today."

The guests then wanted to ask me some questions about the flourless torte. Part of its charm is that you bake it immediately before serving, so it's very warm when they eat it—and for most people, there's not much that beats warm, yummy chocolate goodness.

One of Mrs. Bush's friends said, "Boy! That was great—what all was in there anyway?"

Warm Flourless Chocolate Torte with Raspberry Sauce and Almond Tuile.

I explained how to make it. Everyone thanked me, and I returned to the kitchen. Five minutes later they called me back to the dining room. The same friend of the First Lady said, "Now, please explain to me again how everything goes in there. It was just fabulous. I absolutely adored it!"

It had been a pressure situation—something I didn't often face—especially having to come up with the whole meal and a dessert. This time I managed to hit a home run. Everyone loved the dinner, and the dessert took it over the top with a big finish. It was gratifying to receive the praise, but I don't think I ever got around to telling our pastry chef, Roland, about it.

I came away from that one feeling great! To have the people you serve recognize that you did something extraordinary and thank you for a job well done makes it all worthwhile. And in the shadow of a particularly sad event, I was able to do something good: to bring some joy and comfort to a President's dinner table at the close of a tough day.

In 2004, the Democrats put up Senator John Kerry as a candidate to challenge President Bush. The polls were indicating a close election, and we really couldn't predict the outcome. Once again, we came into November wondering if we'd have a new boss the following year.

When Inauguration Day came around in January 2005, all the staff met the President and First Lady for a welcome-back reception line just as we had for President Clinton. It was a special gathering where we reminisced a little about the first term, offered our congratulations to the President, and reminded the First Couple that we were always there to take care of their needs. Mr. and Mrs. Bush reconfirmed their confidence in our chief usher, and thanked all the staff for our service.

FAREWELL
TO THE
WHITE HOUSE

Farewell

With the return of the First Family, life quickly settled into the same routine. Shortly after the inauguration celebrations had concluded, Executive Chef Walter Scheib was summoned to the chief ushers' office and informed that the President and First Lady had decided they wanted the White House cuisine to go in a different direction during their second term.

On hearing this, Walter offered his resignation immediately. We had no idea what was going on upstairs, so it was a shock when Walter came down to tell us he'd be leaving after eleven years as head chef. He told us he'd resigned voluntarily and that he planned to stay during the lengthy replacement process to help with the workload and smooth the transition.

Finding a replacement for a high-profile job like this is not easy. Once again, we had to go through the same process of selection as when Pierre Chambrin had left — only this time the lengthy background check and security clearance had become much more stringent and time consuming since 9/11.

We couldn't help but wonder what would happen with the rest of us as well. If the First Lady wanted to change direction completely, she just might want to replace the whole staff. It was another reminder that we served "at the President's pleasure."

Our jobs weren't political; we weren't part of the civil-service corps, and we weren't protected by contract or by union. The President could basically do anything he wished to make his and his family's stay in the White House more enjoyable. They clearly wanted to make a change, but we had no idea how deep this change might be — and we wondered who *did* know: The day after Walter resigned, a piece appeared in the *Washington Post* style section. It announced that White House Executive Chef Walter Scheib III was leaving. It offered no details, but we were astounded that word was out so fast.

The next day, Friday, I arrived at midmorning to work the lunch-dinner shift. I found Walter in the office, already packing up his personal effects. I left him and headed to the kitchen. The phone rang there, and I answered a call from *New York Times* food editor Marian Burros, who was looking for Walter. I forwarded the call to him. Walter left at his usual time, and I stayed and worked the evening meal for the First Family.

On Saturday morning, I came in at the same time to work the same shift, and again ran into Walter in the office. He had prepared breakfast and was now continuing his packing. When I went to the kitchen, one of my coworkers asked, "Did you read the *New York Times*?"

"I don't get the *Times*. I get the *Washington Post* at home."

I found a copy of the *Times* and read Marian Burros's article, which described her interview with Walter about his departure. Walter was frank about some things in the interview, and said that he had not resigned, but had been fired for having been unable to "satisfy the First Lady's stylistic requirements." The rest of the article reported a number of Walter's comments, and I wondered as I read it what effect the piece would have. I didn't have to wait long.

After I'd served lunch for the President and First Lady, I took a call around two o'clock from Chief Usher Gary Walters. Gary worked regular hours, Monday through Friday. Unless there was a special weekend function, I hardly ever saw or heard from him on a weekend. In all my years there, this was the only time he'd ever called me from his home on a Saturday. "So, John," he began, "did you have a chance to read the *New York Times* article about Walter?"

"Yes, I did."

"Well," he continued, "so did the administration, and they're not very happy about it. Walter won't be allowed to come back. He's considered a 'Do Not Admit.'"

As that sank in, Gary went on: "The next thing I need to tell you is that the whole kitchen is on you now. You're second in charge, so it's all up to you."

"Well, sure," I replied. "I'm here to do whatever's needed. I'll move forward."

Remembering that Walter had scheduled a tasting on Monday for the upcoming Governors' Dinner and had planned to come in Sunday to prep for it, I reminded Gary about it: "Well, Monday we still have the tasting for the Governors' Dinner."

"Nothing's going to change," said Gary. "That's still going to happen." He went on to talk about another lunch coming up the next week; nothing was supposed to change.

"Fine," I said. "I don't know what Walter had in mind for that lunch, but I'll work to make sure that we have all the ingredients for the menu, and I'll have the platter ready for the tasting."

"You know, John," Gary said reassuringly, "you can do whatever you want at this point. You can change the menu a little, or you can start from scratch if you want."

"Thank you, sir," I said. "Right now I'd like to look at the ingredients we've already received and recreate my interpretation of that menu."

And that was how I became acting head chef at the White House. I stayed late on Saturday and started to work on the ideas behind Monday's tasting. I came in extra early on Sunday, too. Cris Comerford was off that weekend, so I had to work a double shift. I called in some additional staff, and we got busy on the tasting menu. The tasting went well. We made a few adjustments, and everyone was happy with the results. Also, they were very happy with the Governors' Dinner a couple of weeks later.

In fact, things went so well that I decided, after a month, to go and talk to Gary Walters. "Hey, Gary," I began, "I'm kind of curious: what's going on with finding a new head chef? It's been four weeks since Walter left, and I've yet to hear of any candidates to come in for interviews or tastings. Even the press has been quiet."

"To be honest, John, they're really very happy right now." He went on to explain that the President and First Lady were content with how things were going, and that they were extremely busy with other issues during those first weeks of the new term. "Finding a new chef isn't a big priority for them right now. Just keep doing what you're doing."

I told Gary I appreciated the encouragement and was glad to know that things were going so well. "Since you've had a chance to see what I've done in this position, would it be possible for me to put my own name in the hat?"

"Oh, without a doubt!" he said. "You'd be more than welcome to be considered as a candidate. Get your résumé together, give one copy to me, and give one to Social Secretary Lea Berman. We'll review yours, along with all the other candidates'. But for now, just keep doing what you're doing."

Dinner
Honoring
The Governors of the States and Territories

Wild Rice Soup with Pheasant
Patz & Hall Chardonnay "Alder Springs" 2003

Tenderloin of Beef in a Texas Marinade
Spinach and Sweet Potato Batonnets
Spring Vegetable Ragout
Caymus Cabernet "Napa" 2002

Mâche and Peppercress Salad
Baked Brie

"American Pie"
Wild Raspberry-Apple Pie
Cinnamon Ice Cream
Bonny Doon Muscat "Vin de Glaciere" 2003

The White House   *Sunday, February 27, 2005*

Menu for dinner honoring the
Governors of the States and Territories.
February 27, 2005.

March was much like February, except even busier. We continued to make it work with two chefs, and we still didn't hear a peep about the search for a new executive chef. I decided to go see Gary Walters again. "Hey, Gary, we're at two months now, and I still haven't seen any sign of the candidate process starting."

Gary just reiterated what he'd said a month earlier: things were going well; everyone seems very happy, and they don't feel much pressure to get a new chef. He said, "I recommend you keep doing what you're doing."

I didn't argue. I just went ahead and kept things going. After dinner a week later, Mrs. Bush stopped me on the second floor. "I know this has been a lot of extra work for you and Cris," she said. "I just wanted to take a moment to thank you for everything you've been doing lately."

I have to admit, that little encounter recharged my batteries a bit. A pat on the back and a sincere thank-you help to keep you moving forward. It was only a couple of weeks later that we started to see evidence that the chef-selection process was about to get underway. We heard about candidates from all over—one from Rhode Island, one from Texas, and one from Georgia. Each came to do a tasting and sit for an interview, going through their paces to try out for the position. They did small meals and receptions for the President, the First Lady, and the social office to demonstrate their abilities and cooking philosophies. After the candidates' visits, it got real quiet again. Time passed, and we continued to work hard to meet all the requirements of the social calendar.

May was just around the corner—another very busy month at the White House. We had more outdoor events as well as a busy indoor schedule. We began the month with a big Cinco de Mayo party and followed it with a typically busy June.

Then we headed into summer, still wondering. Of course, the news outlets had picked up on the several candidates who'd come in earlier, and there was speculation about who the next head chef might be. Some articles expressed certain points of view. For example, a group of women chefs, Les Dames d'Escoffier International (LDEI), published an editorial expressing their belief that it was time we had a female chef in the White House. As a matter of fact, however, we already had a fine female chef on staff: Cristeta Comerford.

In midsummer, when the social calendar started to quiet down, the social secretary's office decided to bring back two of the chef candidates. Each of them presented another tasting, and we were assured that the administration was "close to making a selection." July came and went, but still no decision was announced. Finally, in mid-August, while I was on vacation, Gary Walters called me to let me know they had made a decision: the new executive chef would be Cris Comerford.

Naturally, I was disappointed, but I was glad that they had decided to promote from within. Cris and I had worked closely together for quite a few years, and keeping it "in-house" allows for continuity. Also, it was great to see a woman appointed to the position of White House Executive Chef for the first time.

MOVING ON

When I returned from vacation, we started to transition to the new era under Cris's leadership, and by the time we'd worked through September and October, I began to recognize that Cris was moving in a new direction.

I began to weigh my options and to think about my own career and what I wanted for the future. I had grown greatly as a chef since joining the White House staff, and had especially enjoyed the additional responsibility of the past few months while in the role of acting head chef. And, although it was difficult, I felt that Cris deserved a chance to select and develop her own staff. She could move in a fresh direction without having to deal with another chef's views.

I finally concluded that it was time for me to leave, so I submitted my notice at the end of November, and began the process of exiting the White House.

It was a tough decision, and not one I took lightly. I had spent over thirteen years as a sous-chef—more than a sous-chef. I enjoyed working in a kitchen that operated with a philosophy that gave full control to whichever chef had responsibility for a particular function. It was like being "Chef of the Day." If Walter put any of us in charge of an event, he acted like their sous-chef and not like the boss. He would come and ask what I needed from him next. He groomed us well to step into the top position, involving us in the whole planning process, from initial notification to working with the administration and dealing with guests' dietary considerations. By delegating those responsibilities to each of us, every chef was up to speed on how it all worked.

I was not only going to miss that kind of work environment, but also would miss working with the First Family. I got to know them so well that I could eventually anticipate what they wanted for lunch—almost before they knew it themselves. I can't really describe how it worked, but I was almost always right about what the family needed on any given day. I would think, *Today is the right day for a chicken tortilla soup,* or *This is a fine day for mushroom soup or a fresh taco,* and after lunch, they'd say, "Great! That really hit the spot."

PROGRAM

INTRODUCTION
JACI VELASQUEZ

SELECTIONS BY
CHRISTIAN CASTRO

SELECTIONS BY
**MARIACHI SOL DE MEXICO
DE JOSE HERNANDEZ**

DINNER

CHILLED AVOCADO SOUP
SERRANO-FLAVORED CRAB MEAT
VINE CLIFF CHARDONNAY "BIEN NACIDO" 2002

CHIPOTLE-RUBBED BEEF TENDERLOIN
GRILLED SQUASH AND BLACK BEANS
RIDGE ZINFANDEL "GEYSERVILLE" 2002

TOMATO & QUESO FRESCA
MESCLUN GREENS
ROASTED CORN DRESSING

CARAMEL FLAN
WARM SAUTÉED BANANAS
MEXICAN WEDDING COOKIES
BLACK STAR FARMS "SIRIUS MAPLE" N/V

**MS.
DOMINGUEZ**

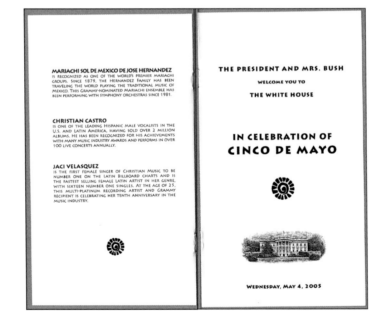

MARIACHI SOL DE MEXICO DE JOSE HERNANDEZ
IS RECOGNIZED AS ONE OF THE WORLD'S PREMIER MARIACHI GROUPS. SINCE 1879, THE HERNANDEZ FAMILY HAS BEEN TRAVELING THE WORLD PLAYING THE TRADITIONAL MUSIC OF MEXICO. THIS GRAMMY-NOMINATED MARIACHI ENSEMBLE HAS BEEN PERFORMING WITH SYMPHONY ORCHESTRAS SINCE 1981.

CHRISTIAN CASTRO
IS ONE OF THE LEADING HISPANIC MALE VOCALISTS IN THE U.S. AND LATIN AMERICA, HAVING SOLD OVER 2 MILLION ALBUMS. HE HAS BEEN RECOGNIZED FOR HIS ACHIEVEMENTS WITH MANY MUSIC INDUSTRY AWARDS AND PERFORMS IN OVER 100 LIVE CONCERTS ANNUALLY.

JACI VELASQUEZ
IS THE FIRST FEMALE SINGER OF CHRISTIAN MUSIC TO BE NUMBER ONE ON THE LATIN BILLBOARD CHARTS AND IS THE FASTEST SELLING FEMALE LATIN ARTIST IN HER GENRE, WITH SIXTEEN NUMBER ONE SINGLES. AT THE AGE OF 25, THIS MULTI-PLATINUM RECORDING ARTIST AND GRAMMY RECIPIENT IS CELEBRATING HER TENTH ANNIVERSARY IN THE MUSIC INDUSTRY.

THE PRESIDENT AND MRS. BUSH

WELCOME YOU TO

THE WHITE HOUSE

**IN CELEBRATION OF
CINCO DE MAYO**

WEDNESDAY, MAY 4, 2005

Dinner menu and program for Cinco de Mayo
celebration at the White House.
May 4, 2005.

Pleasing the First Family and providing them with what they needed was one of the biggest thrills of doing what I did. I had fed the most powerful people in the world—and made them happy. That was enormously satisfying to me for many years.

One More Christmas

After my last day, shortly before Christmas, I received an invitation to the White House Staff Christmas Party. I didn't respond right away and set it aside to think about it. Then, Worthington White, one of the ushers, called me at home: "Hey, are you coming to the staff party?"

"Ah, I don't know," I replied. "Maybe not. I think it's easier to just let it end, you know?"

"Well, did you get an invitation in the mail?"

"Yes."

"You know, if you got an invitation in the mail, it means the President and First Lady would like to have you there."

"I didn't really think about it that way—maybe I should come."

"Well, please do! A lot of people here feel they didn't have the chance to say a proper goodbye to you. I think maybe it would be wise for you to come back just for that—if you want to."

The more I thought about it, the more I realized that Worthington was right. Finally, I decided: "What the heck—I'll do it."

A few days later, my family and I headed to the White House for the staff Christmas party—and I'm so glad we did! When we arrived, we lined up with the other staff families to have our photo taken with the President and First Lady. They were set up in the Diplomatic Reception Room on the first floor, so they were positioned around the corner from where we waited. When we came into view, Mrs. Bush looked my direction and her face just lit up. I extended my hand to her and said, "Hi. How are you doing?"

She reached out with both arms and gave me and my family big hugs. We got into position and posed for our very last Christmas photo with the First Family. It's a treasured memento, to say the least.

President George W. Bush and First Lady Laura Bush were a great, gracious family to work for. (All of the first families I served were wonderful.) In that moment I was delighted that I'd accepted the invitation to the staff party.

Christmas portrait, 2005.
President George W. Bush and Mrs. Laura Bush with (from left)
Alexander Moeller, John Moeller, Zachary Moeller, and Mrs. Suryati Moeller.

What a wonderful way to finish my time at the White House! Attending the party gave me one last chance to visit with coworkers and friends I'd grown to appreciate over the years. I think we talked to everyone that night, and Cris and I had a nice, long chat, which provided us a good, healthy closure.

AN EXIT PHOTO

After the Christmas party, I returned to the White House one more time. Chief Usher Gary Walters phoned me at home to say that the President wanted me to come down to the Oval Office to do an exit photo with him.

In all my years at the White House, I'd never heard of an exit photo. "Gary, what's an exit photo?"

"Sometimes," Gary explained, "the President invites people who've worked at the White House for a long time to come to the Oval Office for one last picture with him before they depart."

"That's cool," I said.

We were given a Tuesday-afternoon appointment, so my wife and I took the boys out of school and went to see the President. After they cleared us to enter the West Wing, we walked down to the Oval Office. After a few moments, President George W. Bush walked in and greeted us. We talked a bit about my departure and my future plans.

Then the President said, "Ah, John, I'm sure you'll do great out there." He made several more kind comments and concluded, "I'll miss having you around."

The photographer took a whole bunch of pictures with the President and our family. What a great experience for us—especially for my sons!

Farewell photograph. President George W. Bush with John Moeller,
Zachary Moeller, Mrs. Suryati Moeller, and Alexander Moeller.
December 2005.

CONTENTS

SOUPS & SALADS

MAINS

Artichoke & Leek Soup

Serves 6 • Preparation Time: 45 minutes • Cook Time: 30 minutes

Chef's Notes: I first made this soup when I lived in the Brittany region of France, where there were hundreds of acres of artichokes, and I always tried new things with them. The idea of pairing artichokes and scallops occurred to me when I was on Nantucket Island, Massachusetts, during the opening day of the scallop harvest. They are some of the best scallops I have ever tasted.

This seemed like an ideal dish for this occasion since I wanted to serve something unique and hopefully different for both presidents to taste. We were in the fall of the year, when artichokes are abundant and the Nantucket bay scallop season had just opened.

Canola oil

¼ cup julienned leeks, cut into 1-inch lengths (for garnish, optional)

5 tablespoons unsalted butter

1 medium leek, white part only, small dice

3 garlic cloves, minced

5 large artichoke bottoms, medium dice, reserved in lemon water

1 medium Yukon Gold potato, peeled, small dice, reserved in water

5 cups chicken broth

½ cup heavy cream

1 tablespoon chopped fresh chives (for garnish, optional)

Salt and fresh-milled black pepper

Heat 3 inches of canola oil in a heavy pan to 320°F. Stirring constantly, place leeks in hot oil, and fry for 2 to 3 minutes, until golden brown. Drain on paper towels, season with fine salt, and set aside.

Melt butter in medium sauté pan over medium heat. Add leeks, and sweat for 4 to 5 minutes. Add the garlic, and stir for another minute. Drain artichokes and potatoes, add to pan, and cook for 5 minutes, stirring occasionally. Add

4 cups of the chicken broth, season with salt and pepper, and simmer for 15 minutes. Remove from heat, and purée mixture with an immersion blender.

Return to heat, add the cream, and simmer for a few minutes, stirring frequently. Check the consistency, and add some of the remaining chicken broth, if soup is too thick. Decrease heat to low, and let stand until ready to serve.

Nantucket Bay Scallops

Serves 6 • Preparation Time: 5 minutes • Cook Time: 4 minutes

Chef's Note: If Nantucket bay scallops are not available, substitute dry-packed bay or small sea scallops.

30 Nantucket bay scallops

2 tablespoons grape seed or canola oil

Salt and fresh-milled black pepper

Season scallops with salt and pepper. Heat oil in nonstick pan over medium-high heat. Place scallops in pan, and sear 1 to 2 minutes per side.

To Plate:

Ladle soup into shallow soup bowls, place scallops in center, and garnish with chives and crispy leeks.

Pan-Seared Poussin with Tarragon-Scented Au Jus,
Corn & Morel Mushroom Custard,
and Green Beans & Pearl Onions

Corn & Morel Mushroom Custard

Serves 6 • Preparation Time: 30 minutes • Cook Time: 40 minutes

Chef's Note: Morel mushrooms are mainly available in the spring. You can substitute any wild mushroom, such as hedge hog, oyster, or shiitake if they are unavailable.

4 teaspoons unsalted butter, plus more for greasing

1 ear of fresh corn, cut off the cob

1 cup fresh small dice Morel mushrooms

2 large eggs and 1 egg yolk

1 cup heavy cream

½ teaspoon minced fresh garlic

1 tablespoon chopped fresh chives

Salt and fresh-milled black pepper

Hot water

Preheat oven to 350°F. Grease 6 (2-ounce) soufflé cups or ramekins with butter, and set aside.

Melt 2 teaspoons butter in small sauté pan over medium heat. Add corn, and sauté for 2 minutes. Remove from heat, and season lightly with salt and pepper. Set aside to cool.

In separate small sauté pan, melt remaining butter over medium heat. Add mushrooms, and sauté for 2 minutes. Remove from heat, and season lightly with salt and pepper. Set aside to cool.

In medium bowl, whisk the eggs and egg yolk together, add cream, continue to whisk, stir in garlic, and season with salt and pepper.

Fill each soufflé cup ⅓ full with custard. Gently combine corn, mushrooms, and chives. Stir 1 teaspoon of mushroom mixture into each soufflé cup. Fill soufflé cups with remaining custard.

Place the soufflé cups in a 6 by 9-inch cake pan. Pour enough hot water into pan to cover ½ of soufflé cups.

Bake 30 to 40 minutes, until custard is firm to the touch. Remove pan from the oven, cover, and allow to rest 20 minutes, before removing custard from cups.

Green Beans & Pearl Onions

Serves 6 • Preparation Time: 15 minutes • Cook Time: 20 minutes

1 tablespoon salt

1 pound French green beans, trimmed

20 pearl onions, peeled

2 tablespoons unsalted butter

Salt and fresh-milled black pepper

Fill large pot with water, add salt, and bring to boil. Plunge beans into boiling water, and boil for 2 to 3 minutes, until just tender. Transfer beans to a bowl of ice water, and drain when cool.

Return water to boil. Plunge onions into boiling water, and boil for 3 to 4 minutes. Transfer onions to a bowl of ice water, and drain when cool.

In medium sauté pan, melt 1 tablespoon butter over medium heat, add onions, and sauté until lightly browned. Season with salt and pepper.

In separate sauté pan, melt remaining butter over medium heat, add green beans, and sauté until heated through. Season with salt and pepper.

Pan-Seared Poussin with Tarragon-Scented Au Jus

Serves 6 • Preparation Time: 45 minutes • Cook Time: 30 minutes

Chef's Note: Poussin is a young chicken, less than 28 days old at slaughter. I've substituted regular chicken breasts for this dish because Poussin is not readily available and requires advanced butchering skills for the dramatic presentation.

1 tablespoon canola oil

6 (5-ounce) boneless chicken breasts

¼ cup dry white wine

1 cup prepared demi-glace

2 tablespoons chopped fresh chives

1 ½ teaspoons chopped fresh tarragon

Salt and fresh-milled black pepper

Heat oil in large sauté pan over medium-high heat. Season chicken breasts with salt and pepper, and sauté 3 to 4 minutes per side, until nicely browned. Transfer chicken to a plate to rest.

Deglaze the pan with the wine. When the wine is reduced by ⅔, add the demi-glace, and reduce by ¼. Stir in chives and tarragon. Season with salt and pepper.

To Plate:

Run a knife around edge of soufflé cup to release custard, and invert onto plate. Arrange beans and pearl onions next to the custard. Place the chicken breast diagonally on plate, and finish with the sauce.

Holiday Dinner Menu: December 2004

Chanterelle Mushroom Soup with Goat Cheese Fritters

Roast Tenderloin of Angus Beef

Black Truffle-Scented Merlot Sauce,
Sautéed Bulb Onions, Herb Potatoes, Green Beans &
Baby Carrots, and Artichokes

Warm Tamale Salad with Avocado, Tomato &
Black Beans and Citrus Dressing

Chanterelle Mushroom Soup
with Goat Cheese Fritters

Goat Cheese Fritters

Serves 6 • Preparation Time: 15 minutes • Cook Time: 5 minutes

¼ cup flour

¼ cup plain, dry fine breadcrumbs

1 egg, whipped with ½ teaspoon water

1 (6-ounce) log goat cheese, sliced into 6 pieces

¼ cup canola oil

Salt and fresh-milled black pepper

Place flour in small bowl and season with salt and pepper. Place breadcrumbs in separate small bowl and season with salt and pepper. Place egg wash in separate small shallow bowl.

Dredge cheese in flour, and shake off excess. Dip floured cheese in egg wash, shake off excess, and dredge in breadcrumbs. Transfer to a plate, and set aside until all cheese slices are breaded.

Heat oil in small sauté pan to medium-high heat. Fry fritters 1 minute per side. Drain on paper towels.

Chanterelle Mushroom Soup

Serves 6 • Preparation Time: 30 minutes • Cook Time: 20 minutes

Chef's Notes: Chanterelle mushrooms are one of my favorites. I had this soup for the first time, and I fell in love with it when at a German restaurant on the Rhine River. Shortly afterwards, I was at a friend's home in the Jura Valley region of France, where we found some fresh chanterelles at the local market. I picked them up and made this soup, which we all enjoyed greatly.

Chanterelles are readily available in the fall through December. If they are out of season, you can substitute any wild mushroom, such as hedge hog, oyster, shiitake, or a combination.

2 tablespoons unsalted butter

1 cup small dice leeks, white part only

½ teaspoon minced garlic

½ teaspoon chopped fresh thyme

1 pound chanterelle mushrooms, cleaned and cut into small pieces

2 tablespoons flour

4 cups chicken broth

1 cup heavy cream

2 tablespoons chopped chives (for garnish, optional)

Salt and fresh-milled black pepper

Melt butter in large pot over medium heat. Add leeks, and sweat for 4 to 5 minutes. Add the garlic and thyme, and sauté for 1 minute. Add the mushrooms, and sauté for 5 minutes.

Stirring constantly, gradually add flour. Add chicken broth, bring to boil, and reduce to simmer for 10 minutes.

Using an immersion blender, purée soup until smooth. Add cream, and simmer for 5 minutes. Season with salt and pepper.

To Plate:

Ladle soup into shallow bowls, float 1 fritter in center, and garnish with a pinch of chives.

Roast Tenderloin of Angus Beef,
Black Truffle–Scented Merlot Sauce,
Sautéed Bulb Onions, Herb Potatoes,
Green Beans & Baby Carrots, and Artichokes

Roast Tenderloin of Angus Beef

Serves 6 • Preparation Time: 30 minutes • Cook Time: 60 minutes

Chef's Notes: Beef filet is always popular at the holidays, so I made this for the Holiday Dinner. It was also a favorite of President George W. Bush.

The tenderloin can be seared the day before roasting. Remove roast from the refrigerator, and let stand at room temperature for 1 hour before roasting.

¼ cup canola oil

4 pounds center-cut beef filet

3 tablespoons unsalted butter, room temperature

1 teaspoon chopped fresh thyme

⅛ teaspoon sea salt

¼ teaspoon fresh-milled black pepper

Heat oil in large skillet over medium-high heat. Sear filet on all sides, until nicely browned. Remove from skillet, place on baking sheet, and cool in refrigerator for at least 2 hours.

In small bowl, mix butter, thyme, salt, and pepper, until well incorporated. Remove filet from refrigerator, and liberally coat with butter mixture. Let stand at room temperature for 1 hour.

Preheat oven to 350°F.

Place filet on roasting rack on sheet pan, and roast 45 to 60 minutes, or to an internal temperature of 130°F to 135°F for medium rare.

Remove from oven, and rest for 20 minutes before carving.

Black Truffle-Scented Merlot Sauce

Serves 6 • Preparation Time: 10 minutes • Cook Time: 30 minutes

Chef's Note: Fresh or frozen black truffles are very expensive and difficult to find. I suggest using canned or jarred truffles for home use. Truffle butter is also available and will give the black truffle essence, if you whisk a bit into the sauce at the last moment.

1 tablespoon plus 1 teaspoon unsalted butter

2 shallots, peeled and thinly sliced

6 black peppercorns

1 sprig fresh thyme

½ cup merlot wine

1 cup prepared demi-glace

1 teaspoon cornstarch, dissolved in 1 tablespoon water

1 tablespoon black truffle, chopped

Salt and fresh-milled black pepper

In a small saucepan over medium heat, melt 1 tablespoon butter. Sauté shallots for 2 minutes, add peppercorns and thyme, and sauté an additional 3 minutes. Add wine, and reduce by ¾. Add demi-glace, and simmer over medium-low heat for 5 minutes. Season with salt and pepper.

Gradually add cornstarch mixture, and return to boil over medium heat, stirring constantly until sauce coats the back of a spoon. Remove from heat, and strain into another small saucepan.

Heat strained sauce over medium heat, and stir in truffles and remaining butter. Remove from heat, and cover until ready to serve.

Sautéed Bulb Onions

Serves 6 • Preparation Time: 10 minutes • Cook Time: 35 minutes

Chef's Note: Bulb onions are usually available in the spring and have a delicate flavor. You can substitute pearl onions for this dish if bulb onions are not available.

6 small bulb onions

1 tablespoon unsalted butter

Salt and fresh-milled black pepper

Trim most, but not all, of the root from the onions, then peel. Cut onions in half through the root.

Melt butter in sauté pan over medium-low heat. Place onions cut-side down in pan, and cook 8 to 10 minutes, until caramelized to a rich golden brown. Remove from heat, cover, and let stand for 20 minutes. Season with salt and pepper, just before plating.

Herb Potatoes

Serves 6 • Preparation Time: 15 minutes • Cook Time: 15 minutes

12 small new potatoes

6 cups water

1 tablespoon salt

1 tablespoon chopped fresh Italian parsley

2 teaspoons chopped fresh tarragon

1 tablespoon chopped fresh chives

1 tablespoon unsalted butter, room temperature

Salt and fresh-milled black pepper

Place potatoes, water, and salt in large pot, and bring to boil. Decrease to simmer, and cook about 10 minutes, until fork tender. Drain and let stand in colander for 5 minutes. Combine parsley, tarragon, and chives in small bowl. Cut potatoes in half, roll in butter, season with salt and pepper, and toss potatoes with herbs. Keep warm until ready to serve.

Green Beans & Baby Carrots

Serves 6 • Preparation Time: 15 minutes • Cook Time: 12 minutes

6 carrots with tops

6 cups water

1 tablespoon salt

½ pound French green beans, stem ends trimmed

2 teaspoons unsalted butter

Salt and fresh-milled black pepper

Trim all but ½ inch of greens from carrots. Peel carrots, and trim to 2 ½-inch lengths. Using a peeler, round off bottom cut of each carrot. Set aside.

In medium pot, bring water and salt to boil. Place carrots in water, and boil for 6 to 8 minutes, until tender. Remove with slotted spoon, and place in bowl of ice water. Return water to boil, and blanch green beans for 2 to 3 minutes, until tender. Transfer to ice water with carrots. Once cold, drain vegetables, and cut carrots in half lengthwise.

Melt butter in medium sauté pan over medium heat. Add carrots and green beans, gently toss, season with salt and pepper, and sauté until heated through.

Artichokes

Serves 6 • Preparation Time: 20 minutes • Cook Time: 25 minutes

6 cups water

1 tablespoon salt

Juice of ½ lemon

6 baby artichokes

2 teaspoons unsalted butter

Salt and fresh-milled black pepper

In medium pot, combine water, salt, and lemon juice. Cut top ½ inch from each artichoke. Using a paring knife, trim the tough outer leaves from each artichoke. Place trimmed artichoke in lemon water.

Bring pot to boil, decrease heat, and simmer for 10 to 15 minutes, until tender. Drain and let cool. Cut artichokes in half lengthwise, and set aside.

Melt butter in medium sauté pan over medium-high heat. Place artichokes cut-side down in pan, and sauté 3 to 4 minutes, until lightly browned. Season with salt and pepper.

To Plate:

Arrange the potatoes, artichokes, and onions in a small semi-circle just inside the rim of the plate. Perch the green beans and carrots against the potatoes. Place 2 slices of meat in center of plate, and ladle some of the sauce on and around the meat.

Warm Tamale Salad with Avocado, Tomato
& Black Beans and Citrus Dressing

Chef's Note: Two favorites of President George W. and Mrs. Laura Bush were tamales and fresh sliced avocados. I decided to pair those ingredients with seasoned black beans, mesclun greens, and tomatoes to make a salad.

Warm Tamale Salad

Serves 6 • Preparation Time: 45 minutes • Cook Time: 60 minutes

Tamale Filling:

6 dried cornhusks

2 teaspoons unsalted butter

¼ cup small dice sweet onions

1 cup fresh cut corn

2 ancho chilies

Salt and fresh-milled black pepper

Place cornhusks in medium bowl, cover with warm water, and soak for at least 1 hour.

Melt butter in medium sauté pan over medium heat. Add onions, and sauté for 2 to 3 minutes. Add corn, and sauté for 3 to 4 minutes. Remove from heat, season with salt and pepper, and set aside.

Place chilies in medium bowl, cover with hot water, and soak for 10 minutes, until soft. Rinse chilies, discard stems, and remove seeds. Place chilies in a small food processor, and purée into a paste. Add a bit of water, if the mixture is too dry.

Tamale Dough:

¾ cup chicken broth

1 cup masa harina

½ teaspoon baking powder

¼ teaspoon salt

¼ cup olive oil

In small saucepot, heat the chicken broth to simmer. In medium bowl, combine the masa harina, baking powder, and salt. Stir in ½ of the broth, and let the mixture rest for a moment. Blend in oil. Check consistency by feel, and add more broth, if necessary, to form a slightly moist soft dough.

Remove cornhusks from water, dry with paper towels, and lay flat on cutting board. Remove a ⅛-inch strip from the long side of each husk, and set aside. Spread about ¼ cup of the dough into a 3-inch square in the center of the husk, leaving at least a 1 ½-inch border. Smear a little of the chili purée on top of the dough, and top with a heaping tablespoon of the corn mixture. Roll husks into a cylinder, twist ends, and tie off with husk strips.

Place ¼ inch of water in medium pot with steamer basket. Bring water to boil, place tamales in basket, cover, and steam for 10 minutes. Remove from heat, and set aside.

Black Beans:

1 cup dry black beans, soaked overnight

2 bay leaves

1 teaspoon hot sauce

¼ teaspoon cumin

2 teaspoons minced garlic

Salt and fresh-milled black pepper

Drain and rinse beans. Place beans and bay leaves in medium pot, and cover with water. Bring pot to boil, and simmer uncovered for 45 to 60 minutes, until tender. Add hot sauce, cumin, and garlic. Season with salt and pepper, and simmer 3 to 4 minutes. Remove from heat, and let stand for 1 hour. Drain before serving.

Salad:

¼ cup fresh squeezed lime juice

¾ cup extra virgin olive oil

½ teaspoon minced garlic

½ pound mesclun greens, washed and dried

2 ripe avocados, sliced

2 ripe tomatoes, sliced

Salt and fresh-milled black pepper

Mix a pinch of salt and pepper into the lime juice. Whisk in the oil and garlic, and set aside.

Place greens in a medium bowl, and toss with just enough dressing to coat the greens.

To Plate:

Place greens on ⅓ of salad plate. Arrange 2 avocado slices on a plate, and brush with the dressing. Place 2 tomato slices next to avocados, and sprinkle some of the black beans on the salad, avocados, and tomatoes.

Cut open one end of the tamale, and open halfway by rolling the husk back. Place on plate alongside the salad.

STARTERS

Grilled Shiitake Mushrooms, Jonah Crabmeat & Herbs, and Roasted Red Pepper Sauce

Luncheon in honor of
His Excellency Silvio Berlusconi
President of the Council of Ministers
of the Italian Republic

Grilled Shiitake Mushrooms
Jonah Crabmeat and Herbs
Jarlsberg Cheese
Roasted Pepper Sauce

Sautéed Grouper
Basmati and Wild Rice
Asparagus and Baby Carrots
White Wine Sauce

Mesclun Greens
Jicama and Grape Tomatoes
Mustard Dressing

Warm Upside-Down Apple Tart
Almond Ice Cream

Ponzi Reserve Chardonnay 1999

The White House   Thursday, January 30 2003

Menu for Luncheon in honor of His Excellency Silvio
Berlusconi, President of the Council of Ministers of the Italian
Republic. January 30, 2003.

Grilled Shiitake Mushrooms

Serves 6 • Preparation Time: 10 minutes • Cook Time: 10 minutes

3 tablespoons extra virgin olive oil

1 tablespoon minced garlic

¼ teaspoon salt

¼ teaspoon fresh-milled black pepper

24 medium shiitake mushrooms, stems removed

Preheat grill to 500° F.

Combine oil, garlic, salt, and pepper in large bowl. Add mushrooms, and toss to coat. Place mushrooms on grill, rotating frequently, and grill for 2 minutes per side.

Jonah Crabmeat & Herbs

Serves 6 • Preparation Time: 15 minutes • Cook Time: 5 minutes

Chef's Notes: Although Jonah crabmeat is available most times of the year, it may be hard to find in some locations. This crab comes from very deep waters off the coast of New England, and the meat is soft and tender. If you cannot find Jonah crab, substitute lump or jumbo lump blue crab.

The crabmeat and herbs can be prepared early in the day and refrigerated, then finished in the broiler just before serving. Be sure to remove the casseroles from the refrigerator 45 minutes before broiling.

Unsalted butter

1 pound Jonah crabmeat

1 teaspoon finely chopped fresh flat-leaf parsley

1 teaspoon finely chopped fresh chives

1 teaspoon finely chopped fresh tarragon

1 teaspoon finely chopped chervil, optional

Juice of ½ lemon

1 tablespoon extra virgin olive oil

24 grilled shiitake mushroom caps

¼ cup finely shredded Jarlsberg cheese

¼ cup finely shredded Comté cheese

Salt and fresh-milled black pepper

Position oven rack in second position, and preheat broiler to medium heat. Lightly grease 6 individual casserole dishes with butter, and set aside.

Place crabmeat in large bowl, and gently break apart, keeping larger chunks intact. Combine herbs in small bowl, remove 1 teaspoon of herb mixture, and set aside for garnish. Gently toss herbs with crabmeat, and season with salt and pepper. Add lemon juice and oil, and gently toss.

Group 4 mushrooms in the center of each casserole dish bottom-side up. Divide crabmeat mixture between casserole dishes, and layer evenly over mushrooms.

Combine Jarlsberg and Comté cheese in small bowl. Sprinkle a layer of cheese on top of the crabmeat, and broil for 5 to 10 minutes, or until cheese is lightly browned.

To Plate:

Transfer casserole dishes to dinner plates. Drizzle sauce around the edge of the mushrooms and crabmeat. Sprinkle with a pinch of remaining herbs.

Roasted Red Pepper Sauce

Serves 6 • Preparation Time: 15 minutes • Cook Time: 20 minutes

Chef's Note: This sauce can be prepared early in the day or a day ahead of time. Gently reheat over medium-low heat.

1 large red bell pepper

2 teaspoons unsalted butter

½ cup small dice sweet onions

1 teaspoon minced garlic

¼ cup chicken broth

¼ cup heavy cream

Salt and fresh-milled black pepper

Grill pepper over open flame, until skin is charred on all sides. Place in small bowl, cover with plastic wrap, and let stand for 10 minutes.

Scrape skin from pepper, cut pepper in half lengthwise, and remove seeds and stem. Small dice pepper, and set aside.

Melt butter in small saucepot over medium heat. Add onion, and sweat for 4 to 5 minutes. Add garlic, and sweat for 1 minute. Stir in bell pepper, and cook for 1 minute. Add chicken broth, and simmer for 8 to 10 minutes. Season with salt and pepper. Transfer mixture to blender, and purée until very smooth.

Place purée in small saucepot, stir in cream, and bring to simmer for 5 minutes. Remove from heat, check seasoning, cover, and keep warm until ready to serve.

Ragoût of Lobster in Riesling Sauce, Celery Root Purée, and Warm Sliced Cucumber & Spinach

Luncheon
Honoring His Excellency
Gerhard Schroeder
Chancellor of the Federal Republic of Germany

Ragoût of Lobster in Riesling
Celery Root Purée
Warm Sliced Cucumber & Spinach

Roasted Virginia Piedmontese Rib Eye
Cabernet Sauvignon Sauce
Glazed Shallots, Young Green Beans
Chanterelle Mushroom Flan

Mixed Young Greens
Fresh Radish and Fennel Salad
Balsamic Mustard Dressing
Cherry and Banana Strudel
Caramel Ice Cream

KARLY Marsanne 1996
HEITZ "Martha's" Cabernet 1974

THE WHITE HOUSE
Thursday, February 11, 1999

Menu for Luncheon honoring His Excellency Gerhard Schroeder,
Chancellor of the Federal Republic of Germany. February 11, 1999.

Ragoût of Lobster in Riesling Sauce

Serves 6 • Preparation Time: 45 minutes • Cook Time: 60 minutes

Chef's Note: Never return water to a hard boil when cooking lobster, only to a light simmer; otherwise the lobster will become tough.

2 gallons water

1 tablespoon salt

1 cup rough-cut carrots

1 cup rough-cut celery

1 cup rough-cut onions

2 sprigs thyme

1 tablespoon black peppercorns

4 bay leaves

Juice of 1 lemon

6 (1-pound) lobsters

Bring water and salt to boil in large stockpot. Add carrots, celery, onions, thyme, peppercorns, bay leaves, and lemon juice. Return to boil, and decrease heat to simmer for 30 minutes.

Cooking 2 lobsters at a time, plunge lobsters into boiling stock, and simmer for 10 minutes. Remove and place on sheet pan.

Remove meat from tail, claws, and knuckles. Place meat on plate, cover, and set aside to keep warm.

Riesling Sauce

Serves 6 • Preparation Time: 10 minutes • Cook Time: 15 minutes

2 tablespoons unsalted butter

3 shallots, thinly sliced

1 sprig thyme

8 black peppercorns

1 tablespoon flour

1 cup Riesling wine

½ cup heavy cream

1 tablespoon lemon juice

¼ teaspoon salt

Melt butter in medium saucepot over medium heat. Add shallots, and sweat for 4 to 5 minutes. Add thyme and peppercorns, and cook for 2 minutes. Mix in flour, and add wine and cream. Bring to boil, decrease heat, and simmer for 5 minutes, or until thickened.

Strain sauce into another saucepot, and stir in lemon juice and salt. Keep warm, until ready to serve.

Soups & Salads

Lobster Bisque with Pesto Galettes

LUNCHEON

Honoring
The Rt. Hon.
The Prime Minister of the United Kingdom of Great Britain and Northern Ireland
and
H.E. The President of the Commission of the European Communities

Lobster Bisque
Pesto Galettes

Mixed Grill
Potatoes Gaufrettes

Autumn Salad

Fresh Papaya with Guava Mousse
Cookies

Talbott Chardonnay 1988
Château Ste. Michelle Merlot 1985

THE WHITE HOUSE
Friday, December 18, 1992

Menu for Luncheon honoring The Rt. Hon. Prime Minister of
the United Kingdom of Great Britain and Northern Ireland
[John Major]
and
H.E. The President of the Commission of the
European Communities [Jacques Delors].
December 18, 1992.

Lobster Bisque

Serves 6 • Preparation Time: 60 minutes • Cook Time: 2 ½ hours

Chef's Note: This is the classical way of making lobster bisque. Even though this recipe may seem intimidating, the outcome is well worth the effort.

1 ½ cups small dice carrots

1 ½ cups small dice celery

1 ½ cups small dice onions

½ cup dry white wine

1 tablespoon black peppercorns

2 sprigs fresh thyme

4 bay leaves

1 teaspoon salt

2 (1 ½ pound) lobsters

2 tablespoons extra virgin olive oil

1 tablespoon chopped garlic

½ cup cognac

¼ cup tomato paste

¼ cup plus 1 tablespoon unsalted butter

¼ cup flour

¾ cup heavy cream

¼ cup sweet sherry

1 tablespoon chopped fresh chives (for garnish, optional)

Salt and fresh-milled black pepper

Fill large stockpot with water, and add ½ cup carrots, ½ cup celery, ½ cup onions, wine, peppercorns, 1 sprig thyme, 2 bay leaves, and 1 teaspoon salt. Bring to boil, and decrease to simmer for 10 minutes. Plunge 1 lobster into the pot, and simmer (do not return to hard boil) for 12 minutes. Remove lobster, and place on a cutting board in a rimmed sheet pan, to cool and reserve juices.

Remove meat from claws and tail. Small dice lobster, and set aside. Coarsely chop lobster body and shells, place in a bowl, and set aside. Place reserved juices in separate small bowl, and set aside.

Place remaining raw lobster on a cutting board, and hold it down, where the tail joins the body. Place the point of a 10-inch chef's knife between the eyes, and drive the knife in, until it cuts through the head to the cutting board. Cut lobster in half from head to tail. Chop each half into 1-inch pieces. Place lobster pieces and juices in bowl with reserved shells.

Heat oil in medium stockpot over medium-high heat. Add ½ cup carrots, ½ cup celery, and ½ cup onions, and sauté for 2 minutes. Add garlic, and remaining thyme and bay leaves, and sauté for 1 minute. Stirring constantly, add shells and raw lobster, and sauté for 4 minutes. Add cognac, and sauté for 1 minute. Stir in tomato paste and all reserved juices, cover with water, and bring to boil. Decrease heat, and simmer for 2 hours, stirring occasionally.

Using a China cap strainer, strain stock into large bowl, pressing out all liquid from shells. Discard shells, and set stock aside.

Melt ¼ cup butter in medium saucepot over medium heat. Add remaining carrots, celery, and onions, and sweat for 4 minutes. Stir in flour, and cook for 1 minute. Add stock, and bring to boil. Reduce heat, and simmer for 10 minutes, stirring occasionally. Using an immersion blender, purée soup, until very smooth.

Strain soup through a fine mesh strainer into medium pot. Bring to simmer, stir in cream, and simmer for 2 minutes. Season with salt and pepper.

In small sauté pan over medium heat, melt remaining butter, and toss in reserved lobster, until heated through. Stir sherry into soup, just before serving.

Pesto Galettes

Serves 6 • Preparation Time: 15 minutes • Cook Time: 15 minutes

1 egg

1 teaspoon water

Flour

1 sheet puff pastry

½ cup prepared pesto

2 tablespoons grated Parmesan cheese

Preheat oven to 375°F. Line baking sheet with parchment paper, and set aside.

Beat egg with 1 teaspoon water, and set aside. On a floured surface, roll pastry to ⅛-inch thickness. Using a 1 ½-inch-diameter circle cutter, stamp out 12 discs of pastry. Using a pastry brush, lightly moisten the edges of 6 of the discs with the egg wash.

Place ½ teaspoon pesto into center of each of the 6 discs. Divide and sprinkle 1 tablespoon cheese on top of pesto. Top with remaining discs, pinching edges together. Using the point of a paring knife, pierce the center of each galette. Lightly brush each galette with the egg wash and divide and sprinkle remaining cheese on top of each galette. Transfer to baking sheet, and bake for 10 to 15 minutes, until golden brown.

To Plate:

Divide lobster into warm soup bowls, and ladle soup over the top. Garnish with chives. Serve with pesto galettes.

Gazpacho Andalouse with
Tomato Granita and Croutons

DINNER

In honor of
Ambassador Pamela Harriman

Gazpacho Andalouse
Tomato Granita
Croutons

Half Smoked Escalope of Atlantic Salmon
Lime & Ginger Sauce
Potatoes Nest with Spinach
Artichoke Bottom & Serrano Pepper

Mesclun Salad
Aged Balsamic Vinegar Dressing

Kiwi Mousse
Poached Apples
Strawberry Sauce

SANFORD *Chardonnay* 1990

THE WHITE HOUSE
Wednesday, May 19, 1993

Menu for dinner in honor of
Ambassador Pamela Harriman. May 19, 1993.

Gazpacho Andalouse

Serves 6 • Preparation Time: 30 minutes • Cook Time: 60 minutes

4 vine ripe tomatoes, peeled, seeded, and small dice

½ cup small dice sweet onions

⅓ cup small dice green peppers

½ cup peeled, seeded, and small dice cucumbers

1 tablespoon plus 1 teaspoon extra virgin olive oil

2 tablespoons red wine vinegar

3 cloves garlic, minced

¼ cup tomato juice

2 tablespoons thinly sliced green onions (for garnish, optional)

Salt and fresh-milled black pepper

In a small bowl, combine 1 tablespoon each of the tomatoes, onions, green peppers, and cucumbers. Stir in 1 teaspoon olive oil, season with salt and pepper, and set aside.

Combine remaining tomatoes, onions, green peppers, and cucumbers, along with vinegar, remaining olive oil, garlic, and tomato juice in blender. Purée until smooth. Season with salt and pepper. Transfer soup to a bowl, stir in vegetables, and refrigerate, until chilled.

Tomato Granita

Serves 6 • Preparation Time: 10 minutes • Cook Time: 60 minutes

1 vine ripe tomato, peeled, seeded, and small dice

1 tablespoon fresh lemon juice

Salt and fresh-milled black pepper

Place tomato and lemon juice in blender, and purée until smooth. Season with salt and pepper. Pour tomato mixture into a shallow baking dish to ½-inch thickness. Place in freezer, until frozen, about 1 hour.

Croutons

Serves 6 • Preparation Time: 5 minutes • Cook Time: 5 minutes

3 slices firm white bread

1 teaspoon extra virgin olive oil

Salt and fresh-milled black pepper

Preheat oven to 350°F.

Trim crust from bread and discard. Cut bread slices into ¼-inch strips, turn slices, and cut into ¼-inch cubes.

In medium bowl, toss bread cubes with oil, and season with salt and pepper. Place bread cubes on baking sheet in a single layer, and bake for 5 minutes, or until golden brown. Cool before serving.

To Plate:

Ladle soup into chilled bowls. Using a teaspoon, scrape the surface of granita to form small quenelle shape, and place in center of soup. Top with green onions and croutons.

Pheasant Soup with Tiny Raviolis and Pacific Northwest Mushrooms

DINNER

In recognition of The Recipients of the
National Medal of Arts and
The Charles Frankel Prize Awards

Pheasant Soup with Tiny Raviolis
& Pacific Northwest Mushrooms

Wrapped Filet of Halibut with Herbs
Yellow Tomato Salsa
Mini-Pumpkin of Baby Vegetables
Basmati Rice, Bell Pepper & Acorn Squash

Autumn Salad with Sprouts & Asparagus Tips
Aged Sherry Vinegar Dressing

Maple Pecan Ice Cream
Spiced Apple Brandy Sauce
Acorn Cookies

FERRARI-CARANO Chardonnay 1991
SAINTSBURY Pinot Noir 1991
ROEDERER White House Special Extra Dry

THE WHITE HOUSE
Thursday, October 7, 1993

Menu for Dinner in recognition of the recipients of the
National Medal of Arts and The Charles Frankel Prize Awards.
October 7, 1993.

Pheasant Soup

Serves 6 • Preparation Time: 20 minutes • Cook Time: 3 ½ hours

Stock:

1 (2 ½-pound) pheasant

½ cup rough-cut carrots

½ cup rough-cut celery

½ cup rough-cut onions

1 sprig thyme

1 sprig parsley

2 cups chicken broth

Using a boning knife, carefully remove 1 breast from the pheasant, and refrigerate for use in ravioli filling.

Place the pheasant in a medium stockpot, and cover with water. Add carrots, celery, onions, thyme, parsley, and chicken broth. Bring to boil, decrease heat, and simmer for 3 hours.

Strain stock through a fine mesh strainer into a bowl, and set aside. Discard solids.

Soup:

1 tablespoon unsalted butter

½ cup small dice carrots

½ cup small dice celery

¼ cup small dice onions

¼ cup small dice leeks, white part only

Pheasant stock

1 tablespoon finely chopped fresh Italian parsley (for garnish, optional)

Salt and fresh-milled black pepper

Melt butter in medium stockpot over medium heat. Add carrots, celery, onions, and leeks, and sweat for 4 to 5 minutes. Add stock, bring to boil, decrease heat, and simmer for 10 minutes. Season with salt and pepper. Keep warm, until ready to serve.

Tiny Raviolis

Serves 6 • Preparation Time: 60 minutes • Cook Time: 10 minutes

Pasta Dough:

3 cups all-purpose flour

½ teaspoon salt

3 eggs

¼ cup water

2 teaspoons extra virgin olive oil

Combine flour and salt in a medium bowl. Make a well in the center of flour. Beat eggs, water, and oil together, and pour into the well. Stir mixture until dough forms a ball. Turn onto a floured surface, and knead until smooth and elastic, about 8 to 10 minutes. Cover and refrigerate for at least 45 minutes.

Filling:

1 pheasant breast, small dice

1 egg, beaten

¼ cup ricotta cheese

2 tablespoons grated Parmesan cheese

1 pinch salt

1 pinch white pepper

1 tablespoon chopped fresh chives

Flour

1 tablespoon salt

½ teaspoon water

Place pheasant in food processor, and pulse until smooth. Add ½ of beaten egg, ricotta cheese, and Parmesan cheese, and process, until smooth. Add salt and pepper, and process, until well incorporated. Transfer mixture to a medium bowl, and fold in the chives. Refrigerate, until chilled.

Remove dough from refrigerator, and cut ball in half. Cover and reserve the dough you are not immediately using, to prevent it from drying out. Dust the counter and dough with flour. Form the dough into a rectangle, and roll it through the pasta machine 2 or 3 times, at its widest setting. Guide the sheet of dough with the palm of your hand, as it emerges from the rollers. Reduce the setting, and crank the dough through another 2 or 3 times. Continue until the machine is at its narrowest setting. The dough should be paper thin, about ⅛-inch thickness.

Lightly dust counter with flour, and lay out pasta sheet. Drop ½ teaspoon of filling about 1 ½ inches apart on the pasta. Mix into remaining beaten egg. Using a pastry brush, brush egg wash around fillings.

Roll out a second sheet from reserved dough, and place on top of filling. Using an espresso cup, gently press out air pockets around each mound of filling to form a seal. Using a 1-inch round cutter, press out raviolis. Place on a lightly floured plate, and set aside.

Fill medium saucepot ¾ full with water. Add 1 tablespoon salt, and bring to a light rolling boil. Place raviolis in water, and simmer for 5 minutes. Using a spider or slotted spoon, remove raviolis, and place in a bowl of ice water. Once chilled, drain and set aside.

Pacific Northwest Mushrooms

Serves 6 • Preparation Time: 5 minutes • Cook Time: 5 minutes

Chef's Note: Depending on the season, Pacific Northwest mushrooms may not be available. Good substitutions are Hedge Hog, Chanterelle, Oyster, or Lobster mushrooms. A local Shiitake or Hen of the Woods mushroom would also be fine.

1 tablespoon unsalted butter

½ pound mushrooms (may be one variety or a combination), cut into small strips

Salt and fresh-milled black pepper

In medium sauté pan over medium-high heat, melt butter, add mushrooms, and sauté until lightly browned. Season with salt and pepper. Keep warm, until ready to serve.

To Plate:

Just before serving, add raviolis to soup to reheat. Ladle soup with 3 raviolis into warmed soup bowls. Top with a spoonful of mushrooms, and garnish with parsley.

Hubbard Squash & Fennel Soup with Shredded Smoked Great Lakes Whitefish

Luncheon

On the occasion of the presentation of
The Rabin~Peres Peace Prize

Hubbard Squash and Fennel Soup
Shredded Smoked Great Lakes Whitefish

Rack of Lamb filled with Green Chard,
Roasted Peppers, Wild Mushrooms
Wild Rice and Root Vegetables
Mustard Tarragon Sauce

Peppercress and Boston Lettuce
Fresh Celery Hearts
Mandarin Orange, Walnut
and Cranberry Dressing

Dried Pear Cake
Warm Spiced Apple Sauce
Winter Fruits Salad
Almond Meringue Cookies

HAGAFEN "Carneros" Chardonnay 1995

The White House
Friday, November 21, 1997

Luncheon Menu on the occasion of the presentation of
The Rabin-Peres Peace Prize. November 21, 1997.

Hubbard Squash & Fennel Soup

Serves 6 • Preparation Time: 15 minutes • Cook Time: 1 ½ hours

Chef's Notes: You can use a butternut squash for this dish if Hubbard squash is not available.

1 small Hubbard squash, or 1 medium butternut squash

2 tablespoons unsalted butter

2 cups small dice leeks, white part only

1 fennel bulb, small dice (reserve tops for garnish)

4 cloves garlic, minced

8 cups chicken broth

1 cup heavy cream

Salt and fresh-milled black pepper

Preheat oven to 325°F. Line sheet pan with parchment paper, and set aside.

Split squash in half lengthwise. Remove and discard seeds. Place squash flesh-side down on sheet pan. Bake 40 to 60 minutes, until soft. Remove from oven, and let rest for about 20 minutes. Scoop out flesh from squash, place in bowl, and set aside.

Melt butter in soup pot over medium heat. Add leeks, and sweat for 4 to 5 minutes. Add fennel, and sweat for 4 minutes. Add garlic, and sweat for 2 minutes. Add squash and chicken broth. Bring soup to boil, decrease heat and simmer for 10 to 15 minutes. Remove from heat and season with salt and pepper.

In batches, purée soup in blender, until smooth. Check seasoning. Return to simmer, and stir in cream. Simmer for 5 minutes. Keep warm, until ready to serve.

Shredded Smoked Great Lakes Whitefish

Serves 6 • Preparation Time: 10 minutes • Cook Time: 15 minutes

Chef's Note: I had the Great Lakes whitefish specially flown in for this luncheon to accompany the squash soup. This fish is not readily available, so you can substitute it with trout. You can purchase smoked whitefish from a Jewish delicatessen if you do not want to smoke the fish yourself. Gently warm purchased smoked fish, just before serving.

2 fillets of whitefish

2 tablespoons kosher salt

½ teaspoon minced fresh thyme

1 tablespoon brown sugar

¼ teaspoon fresh-milled black pepper

2 tablespoons apple wood chips

Lay fillets on cutting board, and remove pin bones, using tweezers. Combine salt, thyme, brown sugar, and pepper, and sprinkle liberally on fillets.

Place woodchips in bottom of stovetop smoker and preheat according to the manufacturer's directions. When wisps of smoke appear, place fish on smoker rack, cover, and smoke for 10 minutes.

Transfer fish to a plate, and let cool for 5 minutes. Flake fish into spoon-size pieces.

To Plate:

Ladle soup into warm soup bowls. Float a tablespoon of smoked fish in the center of the soup, and top with a fennel sprig.

Caramelized Cauliflower Soup and Leek & Cheese Crisp

LUNCHEON

Honoring His Excellency
Mohammed Hosni Mubarak
President of the Arab Republic of Egypt

Caramelized Cauliflower Soup
Leek and Cheese Crisp

Crusted Halibut with Eggplant
Toasted Couscous
Zucchini Ribbons and Morels
Tomato Cardamom Sauce

Young Greens
Cucumber Mint Dressing
Olive Croutons

Sour Cherry Sherbet
with Almond Cream
Honey Glazed Pistachio Bars

TRUCHARD Chardonnay "Carneros" 1994

The White House
Tuesday, July 30, 1996

Menu for Luncheon honoring His Excellency Mohammed
Hosni Mubarak, President of the Arab Republic of Egypt.
July 30, 1996.

Caramelized Cauliflower Soup

Serves 6 • Preparation Time: 40 minutes • Cook Time: 30 minutes

1 head cauliflower, cored and cut into florets

½ teaspoon salt

3 tablespoons unsalted butter

½ cup small dice onions

2 cups chicken broth

½ cup heavy cream

1 tablespoon chopped fresh chives (for garnish, optional)

Salt and ground white pepper

Place cauliflower in medium soup pot, and cover with water. Add salt, and bring to boil for 5 to 10 minutes, until cauliflower is just tender. Using a spider, remove cauliflower, and set aside. Reserve cooking liquid.

Melt 1 tablespoon butter in medium soup pot over medium heat. Add onions, and sweat for 6 to 8 minutes.

Melt 1 tablespoon butter in a medium nonstick skillet over medium-high heat. When the butter begins to brown, place half the cauliflower in the pan, and sauté, stirring constantly, until lightly browned. Transfer cauliflower to soup pot with onions. Repeat, using remaining butter and cauliflower.

Add chicken broth to soup pot with cauliflower and onions, plus enough cooking liquid to cover the vegetables. Bring to boil, and decrease to simmer for 10 to 15 minutes.

Remove from heat, and purée until smooth, using an immersion blender. Return to heat, bring to simmer, and stir in cream. Season with salt and pepper.

Leek & Cheese Crisp

Serves 6 • Preparation Time: 15 minutes • Cook Time: 20 minutes

Flour

1 sheet puff pastry

1 egg beaten with 1 teaspoon water

2 tablespoons grated Parmesan cheese

1 tablespoon unsalted butter

¼ cup small dice leeks, white part only

Salt and fresh-milled black pepper

Preheat oven to 375°F. Line baking sheet with parchment paper, and set aside.

On a floured surface, roll pastry to ⅛-inch thickness. Using a pastry brush, lightly moisten the pastry with the egg wash. Transfer to baking sheet. Lightly season with salt and pepper. Evenly sprinkle cheese across pastry, and place in refrigerator for 15 minutes.

Cut pastry into 1-inch squares, and return to refrigerator for 10 minutes. Bake pastry 6 to 8 minutes, until golden brown. Remove from oven, and let cool.

Melt butter in small sauté pan over medium heat. Add leeks, and sweat for 4 to 5 minutes. Remove from heat, and set aside.

Split each pastry square in half, fill with leeks, and replace tops.

To Plate:

Ladle soup into warm shallow soup bowls, garnish with chives, and serve with cheese crisp on the side.

Chilled Green Pea Soup
with Ginger Mint Scallions

LUNCHEON

On the occasion of
The White House Conference on
Early Childhood Development & Learning:
What New Research on the Brain Tells Us
About Our Youngest Children

Chilled Green Pea Soup
Ginger Mint Scallions

Basil Chicken
Portabello Mushrooms
Tomato Risotto
Fresh Asparagus

Bibb Arugula and Mache Salad
Roasted Onion Dressing

Blood Orange Burnt Cream
Lemon Ladyfingers

The White House
Thursday, April 17, 1997

Luncheon menu on the occasion of The White House
Conference on Early Childhood Development & Learning.
April 17, 1997.

Chilled Green Pea Soup with Ginger Mint Scallions

Serves 6 • Preparation Time: 15 minutes • Cook Time: 20 minutes

Chef's Notes: I selected this soup in order to take advantage of fresh spring vegetables. I used fresh-hulled English peas, but frozen peas can be substituted for this dish.

2 tablespoons unsalted butter

1 sweet onion, small dice

2 teaspoons minced ginger

1 teaspoon minced garlic

1 pound peas

4 cups chicken broth

2 tablespoons chopped fresh mint leaves

½ cup heavy cream

3 tablespoons thinly sliced scallions, green part only (for garnish, optional)

Salt and fresh-milled black pepper

Melt butter in medium soup pot over medium heat. Add onions, and sweat for 4 to 5 minutes. Add ginger and garlic, and sauté for 2 minutes. Add peas, and sauté for 2 minutes. Add chicken broth, and bring to simmer for 5 minutes. Season with salt and pepper.

Remove from heat, and let cool slightly. Stir in mint. In batches, purée soup in blender, until smooth. Chill soup, until ready to serve. Stir in cream, just before serving.

To Plate:

Ladle soup into chilled shallow soup bowls, and garnish with scallions.

Tomato & Fennel Soup
with Shrimp & Scallops

LUNCHEON
honoring
The Honorable John Howard MP
Prime Minister of Australia

Tomato and Fennel Soup
with Shrimp and Scallops

Grilled Duck Breast with Swiss Chard
Wild Rice and Vegetables
Bing Cherry Brandy Sauce

Salad of Summer Lettuces
Toasted Corn and Cherry Tomatoes
Hazelnut Dressing

Chilled Virginia Melon with White Peaches
Spiced Sweet Muscat Wine Sauce
Caramelized Pin Wheels

Mt. Eden "Estate" Chardonnay 1996

THE WHITE HOUSE
Monday, July 12, 1999

Menu for Luncheon honoring The Honorable John Howard MP,
Prime Minister of Australia. July 12, 1999.

Mâche Salad with Heirloom Tomatoes & Mustard Dressing and Croutons with Warm Goat Cheese

Luncheon

Sweet Potato Soup
Rum Crème

Dover Sole with Tarragon Sauce
Spinach, Artichokes and Morel Mushrooms

Mâche Salad with Heirloom Tomatoes
Warm Goat Cheese
Mustard Dressing

Apricot Upside-down Cake
Chocolate Ice Cream
Hazelnut Sauce

Rochioli Chardonnay "Estate" 2003

The White House
Thursday, January 6, 2005

Luncheon Menu.
January 6, 2005

Croutons with Warm Goat Cheese

Serves 6 • Preparation Time: 5 minutes • Cook Time: 5 minutes

Chef's Note: Goat cheese is difficult to slice with a knife; use dental floss for a better result.

6 thin slices of baguette

1 teaspoon extra virgin olive oil

1 log fresh goat cheese

1 teaspoon chopped fresh thyme leaves

Salt and fresh-milled black pepper

Preheat oven to 350°F.

Trim crust from bread, and discard. Place baguette slices on a small sheet pan, and lightly brush each slice with olive oil. Top with a pinch of salt and pepper. Place in oven, and bake 5 to 7 minutes, until crisp. Remove from oven, and set aside to cool.

Slice cheese into ¼-inch slices, and place on top of each crouton. Season with a pinch of pepper, and sprinkle with a pinch of thyme. Just before serving, bake in oven for 3 to 4 minutes, until cheese is warmed.

Mâche Salad with Heirloom Tomatoes & Mustard Dressing

Serves 6 • Preparation Time: 10 minutes • Cook Time: 10 minutes

Chef's Note: Although mâche greens are becoming more popular, depending on the season, they can still be hard to find. Feel free to substitute your favorite greens for this salad.

1 tablespoon red wine vinegar

1 tablespoon Dijon mustard

½ teaspoon minced garlic

1 teaspoon minced shallots

¼ cup extra virgin olive oil

4 heirloom tomatoes (mixed variety if available)

½ pound mâche greens, washed, dried, and chilled

Salt and fresh-milled black pepper

Whisk vinegar, mustard, garlic, shallots, and a pinch of salt and pepper in a bowl. Slowly whisk in the olive oil, and set aside.

Remove core from each tomato, and slice in half. Making quarter turns, cut each half in ½-inch geometric shapes. Place tomatoes in medium bowl, season with salt and pepper, drizzle with about 1 tablespoon of the dressing, and gently toss to coat.

Place greens in separate medium bowl, and gently hand toss with just enough dressing to coat.

To Plate:

Arrange tomatoes in a circle just inside the rim of a salad plate. Place greens in center of tomato circle, and place warm goat cheese crouton in center of greens.

Mousse of Artichokes & Fine Herbs and Salad of
Red Oak Lettuce & Spring Greens with
Pumpkin Seed & Tomato Dressing

Luncheon

HONORING
THE SPOUSES OF THE
MEMBERS *of the* NORTH ATLANTIC COUNCIL

Mousse of Artichokes and Fine Herbs
Salad of Red Oak Lettuce and Spring Greens
Pumpkin Seed and Tomato Dressing

Atlantic Sole with Asparagus,
Baby Carrots, Spinach Leaves, and Young Peas
Vidalia Onion and Chardonnay Sauce

Rose Petal Sherbet
Bouquet of Spring Fruits
Exotic Fruit Sauce   Grapefruit Madeleine

Macari Chardonnay
"Barrel Fermented" 1997

THE WHITE HOUSE   SATURDAY, APRIL 24, 1999

Menu for Luncheon honoring the Spouses of the Members
of the North Atlantic Council. April 24, 1999.

Tomato Shallot Fondue

Serves 6 • Preparation Time: 15 minutes • Cook Time: 20 minutes

2 tablespoons extra virgin olive oil

3 shallots, thinly sliced

2 teaspoons minced garlic

3 vine ripe tomatoes, peeled, seeded, and small dice

½ cup tomato juice

Salt and fresh-milled black pepper

Heat oil in small saucepot over medium heat, add shallots, and sweat for 4 to 5 minutes. Add garlic, and sweat for 5 to 10 seconds. Add tomatoes, season with salt and pepper, add tomato juice, and bring to simmer for 5 minutes. Remove from heat, and keep warm, until ready to serve.

Balsamic Reduction

Serves 6 • Preparation Time: 10 minutes • Cook Time: 20 minutes

1 cup balsamic vinegar

2 tablespoons raisins

1 sprig fresh thyme

Salt and fresh-milled black pepper

Combine all ingredients in small saucepot. Bring to boil over medium heat, decrease to simmer, and reduce by 90%. Strain reduction through a fine mesh strainer into a small pot, and set aside.

Baby Vegetables

Serves 6 • Preparation Time: 30 minutes • Cook Time: 20 minutes

Chef's Note: Baby vegetables can be hard to find at certain times of the year, so use what is readily available and in season.

6 baby turnips with tops

6 carrots with tops

6 cups water

1 tablespoon salt

6 baby zucchini

2 teaspoons unsalted butter

Salt and fresh-milled black pepper

Peel turnips, and set aside. Trim all but ½ inch of greens from carrots. Peel carrots, and trim to 2 ½-inch lengths. Using a peeler, round off bottom cut of each carrot. Set aside.

In medium pot, bring water and salt to boil. Place turnips in water, and boil for 10 minutes, or until tender. Remove with slotted spoon, and place in bowl of ice water. Return water to boil, add carrots, and blanch for 6 to 8 minutes, until tender. Transfer to ice water with turnips.

Return water to boil, and blanch zucchini 1 to 2 minutes. Transfer to ice bath. Once cold, drain vegetables, cut carrots in half lengthwise, and set aside.

Just before serving, melt butter in medium sauté pan over medium heat. Add vegetables, and gently toss. Season with salt and pepper, and sauté, until heated through. Gently toss vegetables with just enough balsamic reduction sauce to lightly coat.

Grilled Salmon Fillet "Mignon"

Serves 6 • Preparation Time: 15 minutes • Cook Time: 15 minutes

Chef's Note: It is important to make sure the grill is clean and very hot when cooking fish; otherwise, the fish will stick to the grill.

6 (5-ounce) skinless, boneless salmon fillets

2 tablespoons extra virgin olive oil

Salt and fresh-milled black pepper

Preheat grill to 500°F.

Roll each piece of salmon into a tight cylinder, and tie with butcher twine. Coat each piece with olive oil, and season with salt and pepper. Grill 3 to 4 minutes per side. For a dramatic presentation, turn salmon ¼ turn after 1 minute, to create crosshatch grill marks. Let rest 5 minutes. Remove butcher's twine before serving.

Seared Portobello Mushroom

Serves 6 • Preparation Time: 15 minutes • Cook Time: 20 minutes

6 medium portobello mushroom caps

2 tablespoons extra virgin olive oil

Salt and fresh-milled black pepper

Preheat grill to 500°F.

Using a paring knife, trim the veil from each mushroom cap. Coat both sides of mushroom caps with oil, and season with salt and pepper. Rotating frequently, grill mushrooms 3 to 4 minutes per side. Transfer to plate, and keep warm, until ready to serve.

To Plate:

Slice mushrooms into ¼-inch strips, and fan off-center on a warm dinner plate. Ladle fondue in front of mushrooms. Cut salmon diagonally into thirds, and artfully place on the fondue. Arrange vegetables on either side of the salmon.

Osso Buco of Salmon & Diver Scallops with Saffron Clam Broth

Luncheon

Honoring
The Honorable Massimo D'Alema
President of the Council of Ministers
of the Republic of Italy

Osso Buco of Salmon and Diver Scallop
Saffron Clam Broth

Roasted Squab with Brandy and Foie Gras
Whipped Potatoes
Caramelized Shallots and Truffles
Baby Beans and Artichoke

Mesclun Salad Greens
Marinated Grilled Eggplant
Balsamic Dressing

Warm Strawberry Crêpes
Grand Marnier Ice Cream Tulip

Gallo "Estate" Chardonnay 1996

The White House
Friday, March 5, 1999

Menu for Luncheon honoring The Honorable Massimo
D'Alema, President of the Council of Ministers of the Republic
of Italy. March 5, 1999.

Saffron Clam Broth

Serves 6 • Preparation Time: 20 minutes • Cook Time: 20 minutes

1 dozen littleneck clams, washed

½ cup dry white wine

2 teaspoons unsalted butter

1 medium shallot, minced

¼ teaspoon crumbled saffron threads

½ cup heavy cream

1 teaspoon cornstarch, dissolved in 1 tablespoon water

Salt and fresh-milled black pepper

Place clams and ¼ cup wine in small saucepot, cover, and bring to boil. Steam clams for 4 to 5 minutes, or until all clams open. Remove clams, and reserve for another use. Strain broth through a fine mesh strainer to remove grit, and set aside.

Melt butter in small saucepan over medium-low heat. Add shallots, and sweat for 3 to 4 minutes. Add saffron, and cook for another 2 minutes. Add remaining wine, and reduce by 50%. Add reserved clam broth, and bring to boil. Stir in cream, and simmer for 3 to 4 minutes. Stirring constantly, add cornstarch mixture, and simmer until sauce coats the back of a spoon. Season with pepper. Taste sauce, and season with salt, if needed.

Strain sauce through a fine mesh strainer, and keep warm, until ready to serve.

Osso Buco of Salmon & Diver Scallops

Serves 6 • Preparation Time: 30 minutes • Cook Time: 15 minutes

Chef's Notes: This is a play on traditional Osso Buco, which is made with veal. The play is on the presentation rather than the cooking method or ingredients. In this dish, the salmon is wrapped around the scallop to give the appearance of veal Osso Buco: the scallop being the bone, and the salmon being the meat.

Diver scallops are large sea scallops that have been hand-harvested by a scuba diver.

2 cups canola oil

15 sprigs Italian parsley (for garnish, optional)

6 large, dry-packed sea scallops

1 (24-ounce) skinless, boneless salmon fillet

1 tablespoon extra virgin olive oil

1 tablespoon unsalted butter

1 medium zucchini, fine julienned

1 medium yellow squash, fine julienned

1 carrot, fine julienned

Salt and fresh-milled black pepper

Line a plate with a paper towel, and set aside.

Heat oil in medium pot over medium heat to 325°F. In batches of 3 to 4 parsley sprigs at a time, place parsley in oil (caution: the parsley will pop and spit oil after the first 3 seconds), and fry for about 10 seconds. Transfer to paper towel-lined plate, and set aside, until ready to serve.

Preheat oven to 375°F. Line baking sheet with parchment paper, and set aside.

Remove the small side muscle from each scallop, and discard. Cut salmon into 6 (1-inch) wide fillets. Wrap each scallop with a salmon fillet, and secure with a skewer.

Heat olive oil in medium nonstick sauté pan over medium-high heat. Season salmon medallions with salt and pepper. Sear 1 to 2 minutes per side. Transfer to baking sheet, and bake for 5 to 6 minutes.

Melt butter in medium sauté pan over medium heat. Add zucchini, squash, and carrots, and gently sauté 4 to 5 minutes, tossing occasionally. Season with salt and pepper. Keep warm, until ready to serve.

To Plate:

Place salmon-and-scallop Osso Buco in center of warm dinner plate. Ladle sauce around outside of Osso Buco. Arrange vegetables in 3 nests around the edges of the Osso Buco. Place 2 to 3 pieces of fried parsley in center.

Florida Yellowtail Snapper and Sautéed Leeks with Saffron Corn Sauce

LUNCHEON
honoring
HIS EXCELLENCY MOHAMED HOSNY MUBARAK
PRESIDENT *of the* ARAB REPUBLIC OF EGYPT

Florida Yellowtail Snapper
Sautéed Leeks
Saffron Corn Sauce

Chicken Breast filled with
Spinach, Almonds and Dried Cherries
Toasted Couscous
Fava Beans and Carrots

Baby Green Sprouts
Parsley, Hearts of Palm and Tomatoes
Lemon Garlic Dressing

Orange and Date Parfait
Chocolate Bars, Almond Meringues and Assorted Melons
Kiwi Sauce

Au Bon Climat
"Talley's Reserve" Chardonnay 1996

THE WHITE HOUSE
Thursday, July 1, 1999

Menu for Luncheon honoring His Excellency Mohammed
Hosny Mubarak, President of the Arab Republic of Egypt.
July 1, 1999.

Saffron Corn Sauce

Serves 6 • Preparation Time: 10 minutes • Cook Time: 20 minutes

Chef's Note: I made this recipe using fresh fish stock that I made from the bones of the yellowtail snapper. Since fish bones can be hard to come by, I've substituted clam juice for this recipe. This recipe is best made with fresh corn; use frozen corn as a substitute if fresh corn is not available.

1 tablespoon unsalted butter

1 tablespoon minced shallots

1 pinch saffron

½ cup fresh corn

½ cup clam juice

¼ cup heavy cream

1 teaspoon cornstarch, dissolved in 1 tablespoon water

Salt and fresh-milled black pepper

Melt butter in small saucepot over medium heat. Add shallots, and sweat for 4 to 5 minutes. Add saffron, and sweat for another minute. Add corn, and sweat for another 4 to 5 minutes.

Stir in clam juice, and bring to boil. Add cream, and boil for 2 minutes. Gradually add cornstarch slurry, stirring constantly, until mixture returns to simmer. Simmer for 4 minutes. Check seasoning, and season with pepper and salt, only if needed. Remove from heat, cover, and keep warm until ready to serve.

Sautéed Leeks

Serves 6 • Preparation Time: 10 minutes • Cook Time: 10 minutes

1 tablespoon unsalted butter

1 leek, white part only, small dice

Salt and fresh-milled black pepper

Melt butter in small sauté pan over medium heat. Add leeks, and sweat for 4 to 5 minutes. Remove from heat, season with salt and pepper, and set aside.

Florida Yellowtail Snapper

Serves 6 • Preparation Time: 5 minutes • Cook Time: 10 minutes

Chef's Note: Yellowtail snapper is found in tropical waters and can be difficult to find, so feel free to substitute red snapper in this dish.

2 tablespoons extra virgin olive oil

6 (4.5-ounce) skinless, boneless snapper fillets

6 snow pea shoots (for garnish, optional)

Salt and fresh-milled black pepper

Heat oil in medium nonstick pan over medium-high heat. Season snapper with salt and pepper, and sear 2 to 3 minutes per side. Transfer to warm plate, and set aside.

To Plate:

Ladle 4 tablespoons of sauce in center of the plate. Place snapper on top of sauce, and top with leeks and snow pea shoots.

Maritime Halibut, Roasted Tomato, Cipollini Onion, Basil White Wine Sauce, and Roasted Asparagus

Luncheon
in recognition of the members of the
Committee for the Preservation of the White House

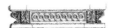

Maritime Halibut
Roasted Tomato   Cipollini Onion
Basil White Wine Sauce

MacRostie Chardonnay 2001

Thyme-marinated Grilled Quail
Multigrain Pilaf
White Asparagus and Leeks

Mesclun Greens
Raspberry Dressing

White House Fruit Basket

The White House   Friday March 12, 2004

Menu for Luncheon in recognition of the members of the
Committee for the Preservation of the White House.
March 12, 2004.

Roasted Tomato

Serves 6 • Preparation Time: 5 minutes • Cook Time: 2 hours

6 vine ripe Roma tomatoes

1 tablespoon extra virgin olive oil

Salt and fresh-milled black pepper

Preheat oven to 270°F.

Core the stem from each tomato. Cut tomatoes in half lengthwise, and place flesh-side up on small roasting rack on a sheet pan. Moisten tomato with oil, and season with salt and pepper. Bake for 2 to 2 ½ hours, until 70% of moisture is evaporated, and tomatoes are lightly browned. Remove from oven, and keep warm, until ready to serve.

Basil White Wine Sauce

Serves 6 • Preparation Time: 10 minutes • Cook Time: 20 minutes

1 cup packed fresh basil leaves

⅓ cup extra virgin olive oil

½ teaspoon minced garlic

¾ cup dry white wine

1 shallot, julienned

2 bay leaves

6 black peppercorns

¼ cup heavy cream

1 stick unsalted butter, room temperature

½ teaspoon lemon juice

Salt and fresh-milled black pepper

Place basil leaves, oil, and garlic into blender. Season with salt and pepper, and purée until just smooth. Transfer mixture from blender to a small bowl, cover with plastic wrap, and set aside.

Combine wine, shallots, bay leaves, and peppercorns in medium saucepot over medium-high heat. Bring to boil, decrease heat to medium, and reduce liquid by 75%.

Stir in cream, and reduce by 50%. Stir in butter, 1 pat at a time, until well incorporated. Stir in lemon juice, and season with salt and pepper. Strain sauce through a fine mesh strainer into a small saucepot. Keep warm over very low heat, stirring occasionally.

Just before serving, stir in 1 tablespoon of the basil purée. Reserve remaining puree for another use.

Roasted Asparagus

Serves 6 • Preparation Time: 5 minutes • Cook Time: 10 minutes

30 pieces asparagus, trimmed to 3 ½-inch lengths

1 tablespoon extra virgin olive oil

Salt and fresh-milled black pepper

Preheat oven to 400°F.

In large bowl, toss asparagus with oil, and season with salt and pepper. Lay asparagus on sheet pan in single layer. Rotating asparagus frequently, roast for 8 to 10 minutes, until tender and lightly browned. Remove from oven, and keep warm, until ready to serve.

Cipollini Onion

Serves 6 • Preparation Time: 5 minutes • Cook Time: 10 minutes

5 cipollini onions, peeled with root intact

1 tablespoon unsalted butter

Salt and fresh-milled black pepper

Cut each onion into eighths through the root. Melt butter in medium sauté pan over medium heat. Just as butter begins to brown, add onions, and sauté for 4 to 5 minutes, or until lightly browned. Remove from heat, and season with salt and pepper. Keep warm, until ready to serve.

Maritime Halibut

Serves 6 • Preparation Time: 10 minutes • Cook Time: 15 minutes

6 (5-ounce) skinless, boneless halibut fillets

2 tablespoons grape seed or canola oil

Salt and fresh-milled black pepper

Preheat oven to 350°F.

Season halibut with salt and pepper. Heat oil in a nonstick pan over medium-high heat. In batches, sear halibut in pan for 2 to 3 minutes per side. Transfer fillets to a sheet pan, place in oven, and bake for 8 to 10 minutes, or until meat thermometer reads 145°F. Remove from oven, and rest for 4 to 5 minutes before serving.

To Plate:

Fan asparagus on one side of a warm dinner plate. Cut roasted tomatoes in half, and arrange next to asparagus. Place onions on top of asparagus, and perch the fish against the vegetables. Ladle sauce over fish.

Braised Rabbit, Saffron Risotto, Acorn Squash, and Ragoût of Tomato, Fennel & Onion

LUNCHEON
honoring
**HIS EXCELLENCY GUILIANO AMATO
PRESIDENT of the COUNCIL OF MINISTERS
OF THE ITALIAN REPUBLIC**

Roasted Monkfish
Applewood Smoked Bacon and Sweet White Corn Sauce
Sautéed Wild Mushrooms

Braised Rabbit
Saffron Rissoto ❖ Acorn Squash
Ragoût of Tomato, Fennel and Onion

Summer Greens
Buffalo Mozzarella Cheese ❖ Roasted Peppers
Tarragon Dressing

Poached Apple in White Wine Jelly
Raspberries and Grapes
Assorted Macaroons

Far Niente Chardonnay 1998

THE WHITE HOUSE
Wednesday, September 20, 2000

Menu for Luncheon honoring His Excellency Guiliano Amato,
President of the Council of Ministers of the Italian Republic.
September 20, 2000.

Braised Rabbit

Serves 6 • Preparation Time: 30 minutes • Cook Time: 30 minutes

6 boneless rabbit legs, butterflied

12 large basil leaves

2 tablespoons unsalted clarified butter

1 shallot, minced

½ cup dry white wine

1 cup chicken broth

2 teaspoons cornstarch, dissolved in 1 tablespoon water

Salt and fresh-milled black pepper

Preheat oven to 325°F.

Season interior of rabbit legs with salt and pepper, and place 2 basil leaves inside each leg. Roll leg closed, and tie with butcher's twine in 3 places. Season with salt and pepper.

Heat butter in large oven-safe sauté pan over medium-high heat. Place rabbit in pan, and brown on all sides, about 5 minutes. Remove rabbit from pan, and set aside. Drain excess fat from pan, add shallots, and sauté for 1 minute. Add wine, and deglaze pan for 30 seconds. Return rabbit to pan, add chicken broth, and bring to boil. Cover, transfer to oven, and bake for 20 to 25 minutes. Transfer rabbit to plate, and let rest for 20 minutes.

Using a fine mesh strainer, strain the cooking liquid into a small saucepot. Bring liquid to simmer, and add any juices from rabbit on plate. Stirring constantly, add the cornstarch mixture, return to simmer, and cook until the sauce coats the back of a spoon. Season with salt and pepper.

Ragoût of Tomato, Fennel & Onion

Serves 6 • Preparation Time: 20 minutes • Cook Time: 20 minutes

1 tablespoon extra virgin olive oil

½ cup small dice sweet onions

1 tablespoon minced garlic

½ cup small dice fresh fennel (reserve tops for garnish)

¼ cup dry white wine

2 large ripe tomatoes, peeled, seeded, and small dice

Salt and fresh-milled black pepper

Heat oil in small saucepot over medium heat. Add onions, and sweat for 1 minute. Add garlic and fennel, season with salt and pepper, and continue to sweat for 4 to 5 minutes. Add wine, and deglaze pan for 30 seconds. Add pan juices, and bring to simmer. Add tomatoes, and cook for 5 minutes. Season with salt and pepper, and set aside, until ready to serve.

Acorn Squash

Serves 6 • Preparation Time: 10 minutes • Cook Time: 10 minutes

Chef's Note: Every summer, I experiment with growing different vegetables in my home garden. I often took the vegetables I grew to the White House and served them to the First Family. One year, I grew an abundance of acorn squash. To try something different, I marinated and grilled the squash and served it to my family and friends. No one knew what it was, but they loved it. I served this to the First Family, and it became a favorite of Mrs. Laura Bush. This is what inspired me to incorporate it into this formal menu for the president of Italy.

1 acorn squash

2 tablespoons extra virgin olive oil

1 teaspoon minced garlic

1 teaspoon herbes de Provence

Salt and fresh-milled black pepper

Cut squash in half, and remove seeds. Cut squash into ¼-inch slices, and peel. Place squash in large bowl, and coat with oil, garlic, and herbs. Season with salt and pepper. Grill over high heat 2 to 3 minutes per side. For a dramatic presentation, turn squash ¼ turn after 1 minute, to create crosshatch grill marks.

Saffron Risotto

Serves 6 • Preparation Time: 15 minutes • Cook Time: 40 minutes

4 cups chicken broth

2 tablespoons unsalted butter

⅓ cup chopped sweet onions

2 teaspoons minced garlic

¼ teaspoon crumbled saffron threads

1 cup Arborio rice

¼ cup grated Parmesan cheese

Salt and fresh-milled black pepper

In medium pot, heat chicken broth to simmer. Melt 1 tablespoon butter in small saucepot over medium heat. Add onions, and sweat for 4 to 5 minutes. Add garlic, and sweat for 2 minutes. Add saffron, and sauté for 2 minutes. Add rice, season with salt and pepper, and sauté for 1 minute.

Stirring constantly, add ½ cup chicken broth. As rice absorbs the liquid, continue to add broth ¼ cup at a time. Once all broth is added, decrease heat to low simmer, and continue to cook for 30 minutes, stirring occasionally. When rice is tender, remove from heat, and let stand for 5 minutes. Stir in remaining butter and cheese. Add more broth, if needed, for a creamy consistency. Season with salt and pepper.

To Plate:

Place risotto on plate, cut squash crescents in half, and fan next to risotto. Using a slotted spoon, place a spoonful of ragoût alongside the risotto. Remove string from rabbit, slice each leg into 4 or 5 slices, and fan on plate next to risotto and vegetables. Spoon sauce over rabbit, and top with a sprig of fennel top.

LUNCHEON HONORING
HER EXCELLENCY
Megawati Soekarnoputri
PRESIDENT of the REPUBLIC of INDONESIA

Yellowtail Snapper
Basil AND Carrot Risotto
Fennel Pepper Coulis

Herb Crusted Chicken Breast
Chanterelle Mushroom
Roasted Eggplant, Zucchini AND Tomato

Boston Greens
Artichoke AND Hearts OF Palm
Balsamic Dressing

Papaya WITH *Lime Mousse*
Strawberry Sauce

Navarro Pinot Gris 2000

THE WHITE HOUSE
WEDNESDAY, SEPTEMBER 19, 2001

Menu for Luncheon honoring Her Excellency Megawati
Soekarnoputri, President of the Republic of Indonesia.
September 19, 2001.

Herb–Crusted Chicken Breast, Chanterelle Mushrooms, and Roasted Eggplant, Zucchini & Tomato

Herb-Crusted Chicken Breast

Serves 6 • Preparation Time: 30 minutes • Cook Time: 30 minutes

Chef's Note: I was always looking for interesting light fare to make for lunch. This idea came from a restaurant that I worked at in France, Chez Camille. I thought that if I could crust the chicken with this wonderful mixture of herbs, it would not only give a dramatic presentation, but it would taste great also. This combination of herbs is known as fine herbs and blends together well. I'm always looking to create new ways to prepare chicken. Now 1,002 ways to cook chicken!

1 teaspoon finely chopped fresh flat-leaf parsley

1 teaspoon finely chopped fresh chives

1 teaspoon finely chopped fresh tarragon

1 teaspoon finely chopped chervil, optional

¼ cup flour

¼ teaspoon salt

¼ teaspoon pepper

6 (5-ounce) skinless, boneless chicken breasts

1 egg white, lightly whipped

¼ cup unsalted clarified butter

Preheat oven to 350°F.

Combine parsley, chives, tarragon, and chervil in shallow bowl. Place flour in separate small bowl, and stir in salt and pepper. Dredge skin side only of chicken breast in flour, and shake off excess. Dip floured side of chicken in egg white, and shake off excess. Place chicken breast on plate, floured-and-egg side up. Evenly sprinkle chicken with fine herb mixture.

Heat medium sauté pan over medium-high heat, and add clarified butter. In batches, place chicken herb-side down in pan, and gently sauté 4 to 5 minutes per side. Transfer to sheet pan herb-side up, and finish in oven for 8 to 10 minutes. Remove from the oven, and let it rest for 5 minutes.

White Wine Butter Sauce

Serves 6 • Preparation Time: 10 minutes • Cook Time: 20 minutes

½ cup dry white wine

1 shallot, peeled and sliced

6 black peppercorns

2 bay leaves

½ cup heavy cream

2 sticks unsalted butter, room temperature

Juice of ½ lemon

Salt and fresh-milled black pepper

In small saucepot over medium-high heat, combine wine, shallots, peppercorns, and bay leaves, and bring to simmer for 10 to 12 minutes, or until reduced by 90%. Add the cream, and continue to simmer for 5 minutes, or until reduced by 50%. Decrease heat to medium low, and whisk in the butter, 1 tablespoon at a time. Stir in lemon juice, and season with salt and pepper. Strain through a fine mesh strainer into another small saucepot, and keep warm over low heat. Do not boil (the sauce will separate).

Chanterelle Mushrooms

Serves 6 • Preparation Time: 5 minutes • Cook Time: 10 minutes

Chef's Note: Chanterelle mushrooms are mainly available in the fall; you can use any wild mushroom as a substitute if they are not available.

1 tablespoon unsalted butter

¼ pound chanterelle mushrooms, cut into ¼-inch pieces

½ teaspoon minced shallots

Salt and fresh-milled black pepper

Melt butter in medium sauté pan over medium-high heat. Add mushrooms, and sauté 3 to 4 minutes. Add shallots, season with salt and pepper, and continue to sauté 2 to 3 minutes, until lightly brown. Remove from heat, and keep warm, until ready to serve.

Roasted Eggplant, Zucchini & Tomato

Serves 6 • Preparation Time: 15 minutes • Cook Time: 15 minutes

1 tablespoon salt

¼ pound yellow beans, trimmed

¼ pound fresh asparagus, trimmed

Extra virgin olive oil

1 Chinese eggplant

1 small zucchini

2 teaspoons minced garlic

1 ripe Roma tomato, peeled and sliced

2 teaspoons unsalted butter

Salt and fresh-milled black pepper

Fill medium pot with water, add salt, and bring to boil. Place beans in pot, and boil for 4 to 5 minutes. Remove beans with slotted spoon, and place in a bowl of ice water. Return water to boil, add asparagus, and boil for 3 to 4 minutes, until tender. Transfer to ice water with beans. Once cold, drain and set aside.

Preheat oven to 400°F. Grease 2 sheet pans lightly with olive oil.

Cut eggplant and zucchini into ¼-inch slices, and arrange on separate sheet pans in a single layer. Lightly spray eggplant and zucchini with olive oil, rub some garlic on each piece, and season with salt and pepper. Bake eggplant for 5 to 6 minutes, and bake zucchini for 6 to 8 minutes.

Top each slice of eggplant with a tomato slice, lightly spray with olive oil, return to oven, and bake for 3 to 4 minutes, or until heated through.

In medium sauté pan, melt butter, and gently toss in beans and asparagus. Season with salt and pepper, and sauté, until heated through. Keep warm, until ready to serve.

To Plate:

Place asparagus and beans on plate, then layer zucchini, eggplant, and tomatoes alongside, and top with a spoonful of mushrooms. Slice chicken breasts, and arrange in a fan across vegetables. Ladle sauce around chicken.

Rosemary & Garlic Roasted Chicken, Ragoût of Summer Vegetables, and Shiitake Polenta with Pan Juices

Luncheon

Honoring
His Excellency
Binyamin Netanyahu
Prime Minister of Israel

Chilled Sunchoke Soup with
Salmon and Watercress

Rosemary & Garlic Roasted Chicken
Ragout of Summer Vegetables
Shitake Polenta with Pan Juices

Salad of Radicchio, Endive
and Frissée with a Basil Oil Dressing
Crispy Sweet Potatoes

Cherry Sherbet with Fresh Peaches
Pistachio Macaroons

(Mt. Madroña Chardonnay 1992)

Tuesday, July 9, 1996   The White House

Menu for Luncheon honoring His Excellency Binyamin
Netanyahu, Prime Minister of Israel.
July 9, 1996.

Rosemary & Garlic Roasted Chicken

Serves 6 • Preparation Time: 30 minutes • Cook Time: 1 ½ hours

3 (3-pound) chickens

3 sprigs fresh rosemary

¾ cup small dice carrots

¾ cup small dice celery

¾ cup small dice onions

6 cloves garlic, sliced

3 lemon halves

1 tablespoon minced garlic

1 tablespoon minced fresh rosemary

1 tablespoon unsalted butter, room temperature

2 tablespoons unsalted butter, melted

Salt and fresh-milled black pepper

Preheat oven to 375°F.

Pat chickens dry with paper towels. Season cavities with salt and pepper. In each chicken, place 1 rosemary sprig, ¼ cup carrots, ¼ cup celery, ¼ cup onions, and 2 cloves of the sliced garlic. Squeeze the juice from ½ of a lemon into each cavity, and place lemon inside.

Combine minced garlic, rosemary, and butter. Gently slide your hand under the skin to loosen the skin from the chicken breast. Smear ⅓ butter mixture per chicken on the breast meat. Truss each chicken with butcher's twine.

Lightly coat the skins of the chickens with the melted butter. Season with salt and pepper. Place chickens in roasting pan with rack, and roast for 20 minutes. Reduce heat to 325°F, and roast for 40 minutes. Remove from oven, transfer chickens to a platter, and let rest for 30 minutes.

Pan Juices

Serves 6 • Preparation Time: 10 minutes • Cook Time: 15 minutes

½ cup dry white wine

2 cups chicken broth

1 tablespoon cornstarch mixed into 3 tablespoons water

Salt and fresh-milled black pepper

Heat roasting pan over medium-high heat. Add wine to deglaze pan, constantly scraping the bottom. Allow wine to reduce by 50%. Add chicken broth and any juices from resting chickens. Bring to light boil, continuously scraping bottom and sides of pan. After 5 minutes, season with salt and pepper, and gradually add cornstarch slurry. Reduce heat, and simmer for 5 minutes, or until the sauce coats the back of a spoon.

Strain sauce through fine mesh strainer into small saucepot. Cover and keep warm, until ready to serve.

Ragoût of Summer Vegetables

Serves 6 • Preparation Time: 20 minutes • Cook Time: 15 minutes

2 tablespoons extra virgin olive oil

1 small onion, medium dice

4 cloves garlic, minced

1 yellow squash, medium dice

1 zucchini, medium dice

1 small eggplant, medium dice

2 ripe tomatoes, peeled, seeded, and medium dice

Salt and fresh-milled black pepper

Heat oil in a medium sauté pan over medium heat. Add onions, and sauté for 1 minute. Stir in garlic, and add squash, zucchini, and eggplant. Sauté for 5 minutes. Stir in tomatoes, season with salt and pepper, and sauté for 3 minutes. Remove from heat, and keep warm, until serving.

Shiitake Polenta

Serves 6 • Preparation Time: 15 minutes • Cook Time: 40 minutes

3 tablespoons unsalted butter

½ cup small dice onions

4 cloves fresh garlic, minced

3 cups chicken broth

1 cup polenta

½ pound shiitake mushrooms, thinly sliced

¼ cup grated Parmesan cheese

Salt and fresh-milled black pepper

Melt 1 tablespoon butter in medium saucepan over medium heat. Add onions, and sweat for 4 to 5 minutes. Add garlic, and cook for 1 minute. Add chicken broth, and bring to boil. Slowly stir in polenta. Return to simmer, and cook for 20 minutes, stirring occasionally. Season with salt and pepper.

Melt 1 tablespoon butter in medium sauté pan. Add mushrooms, and sauté 5 to 6 minutes, until tender. Season with salt and pepper. Remove from heat, and set aside.

Stir remaining butter into polenta. Fold in mushrooms and cheese. Keep warm, until ready to serve.

To Plate:

Carefully remove chicken breasts with wing bone and skin intact. Scoop polenta onto warm dinner plate. Lean chicken breast against polenta. Arrange vegetable ragoût next to chicken. Ladle sauce over chicken. Reserve remaining chicken for another use.

Basil Chicken with Portobello Mushrooms, Tomato Risotto, and Fresh Asparagus

LUNCHEON

On the occasion of
The White House Conference on
Early Childhood Development & Learning:
What New Research on the Brain Tells Us
About Our Youngest Children

Chilled Green Pea Soup
Ginger Mint Scallions

Basil Chicken
Portabello Mushrooms
Tomato Risotto
Fresh Asparagus

Bibb Arugula and Mache Salad
Roasted Onion Dressing

Blood Orange Burnt Cream
Lemon Ladyfingers

The White House
Thursday, April 17, 1997

Luncheon menu on the occasion of The White House
Conference on Early Childhood Development & Learning.
April 17, 1997.

Basil Chicken with Portobello Mushrooms

Serves 6 • Preparation Time: 25 minutes • Cook Time: 20 minutes

6 (5-ounce) boneless chicken breasts, butterflied

12 fresh basil leaves

2 tablespoons grated Parmesan cheese

3 tablespoons extra virgin olive oil

1 tablespoon minced shallots

½ cup dry white wine

1 cup chicken broth

3 basil leaves, minced

1 teaspoon cornstarch, dissolved in 1 tablespoon water

3 portobello mushroom caps

Salt and fresh-milled black pepper

Preheat oven to 350°F.

Lay out chicken breasts, and place 2 basil leaves in each breast. Sprinkle with cheese, season with salt and pepper, and close. Season the outside of each breast with salt and pepper.

Heat 1 tablespoon oil in medium oven-safe sauté pan over medium-high heat. Lightly brown chicken on both sides. Bake in oven for 8 to 10 minutes. Place chicken on plate, and set aside.

Remove excess fat from pan, and place over medium-low heat. Add shallots, and sauté for 30 seconds. Add wine, deglaze pan, then add chicken broth, and reduce by 50%. Stir in minced basil, and season with salt and pepper. Stirring constantly, gradually add cornstarch mixture, and bring to boil over medium heat. Cook until the sauce coats the back of a spoon. Remove from heat, strain into small saucepan, cover, and keep warm, until ready to serve.

In oven-safe sauté pan, over medium heat, sauté mushrooms in remaining olive oil for 2 to 3 minutes per side. Place in oven for 5 minutes, or until tender. Remove mushrooms from pan, and place on plate to cool slightly.

Tomato Risotto

Serves 6 • Preparation Time: 15 minutes • Cook Time: 40 minutes

3 cups chicken broth

2 tablespoons unsalted butter

⅓ cup chopped sweet onions

2 teaspoons minced garlic

1 cup Arborio rice

¼ cup grated Parmesan cheese

2 vine ripe tomatoes, peeled, seeded, and small dice

2 cups canola oil (optional, for garnish)

6 medium-sized basil leaves (optional, for garnish)

Salt and fresh-milled black pepper

In medium pot, heat chicken broth to simmer.

In 2-quart saucepot over medium heat, melt 1 tablespoon butter, add onions, and sweat for 4 to 5 minutes. Add garlic, and sweat for 2 minutes. Add rice, season with salt and pepper, and sauté for 1 minute. Stirring constantly, add ½ cup chicken broth. As rice absorbs the liquid, continue to add broth, ¼ cup at a time. Reduce heat to low simmer, and continue to cook for 20 minutes, stirring occasionally.

When rice is tender, remove from heat, and let stand for 5 minutes. Stir in remaining butter and cheese. Add more stock, if needed, for a creamy consistency. Fold in all but 3 tablespoons tomatoes, and season with salt and pepper.

In medium pot, heat canola oil to 310°F. Add basil leaves, one at a time, and fry for about 10 seconds. Remove from oil, and drain on paper towels. Season lightly with salt.

Fresh Asparagus

Serves 6 • Preparation Time: 5 minutes • Cook Time: 10 minutes

1 tablespoon salt

30 pieces asparagus, trimmed

1 tablespoon unsalted butter

Salt and fresh-milled black pepper

Fill medium pot with water, add salt, and bring to boil. Place asparagus in pot, and boil for 3 to 4 minutes, until just tender. Remove asparagus with slotted spoon, and place in a bowl of ice water.

Melt butter in medium sauté pan, add asparagus, and sauté 2 to 3 minutes, until warm. Season with salt and pepper.

To Plate:

Scoop a portion of risotto onto the center of each plate, and top with remaining tomatoes. Stand one fried basil leaf in tomatoes. Slice each mushroom into 6 slices. Slice chicken breast into thirds. Alternating chicken and mushrooms, place slices against risotto. Ladle sauce over chicken and mushrooms. Arrange asparagus alongside chicken.

Rolled Chicken with Fig & Leek, Tomato Scallion Sauce, Chipotle Chili Polenta, Asparagus, and Baby Carrots

Luncheon

Honoring His Excellency Heydar Aliyev President of the Republic of Azerbaijan

Chilled Zucchini and Summer Squash Soup with Garlic

Rolled Chicken with Fig and Leek
Tomato Scallion Sauce
Chipotle Chili Polenta
Asparagus and Baby Carrots

Field Green Salad
Basil Dressing
Roasted Corn

Fresh Peach Tart
Apple and Raspberry Sherbet
Minted Cinnamon Sauce

SIMI "Sendal" 1993

The White House
Friday, August 1, 1997

Menu for Luncheon honoring His Excellency Heydar Aliyev,
President of the Republic of Azerbaijan. August 1, 1997.

Rolled Chicken with Fig & Leek

Serves 6 • Preparation Time: 3 hours • Cook Time: 30 minutes

Chef's Note: Fresh figs are preferable for this dish, but since the window of availability of fresh figs is so small, I have used dried figs here.

2 tablespoons unsalted butter

½ cup small dice leeks, white part only

8 dried figs, soaked in warm water for 3 hours

6 (5-ounce) boneless chicken breasts, butterflied

2 tablespoons canola oil

Salt and fresh-milled black pepper

Preheat oven to 350°F.

In small sauté pan over medium-low heat, melt 1 tablespoon butter, add leeks, and sweat for 4 to 5 minutes. Season with salt and pepper, and set aside to cool.

Cut figs in quarters, and set aside.

Lay out chicken breast between 2 pieces of plastic wrap, and pound gently to ¼-inch thickness. Place 5 fig quarters on one side of chicken filet, top with 4 teaspoons leeks, and roll chicken into cylinder.

Lay out 6 sheets of aluminum foil, smear lightly with remaining butter, and sprinkle with salt and pepper. Place chicken on foil, roll up, and twist ends tightly to close.

Heat oil in large skillet over medium heat. Place chicken rolls in skillet, and brown on all sides for about 8 minutes. Transfer chicken to a sheet pan, and bake for 10 minutes.

Remove from oven, cut ends off of foil packet, and let rest for 10 minutes before serving.

Tomato Scallion Sauce

Serves 6 • Preparation Time: 20 minutes • Cook Time: 20 minutes

2 tablespoons extra virgin olive oil

2 teaspoons minced garlic

3 vine ripe tomatoes, peeled, seeded, and small dice

½ cup tomato juice

½ cup thinly sliced scallions

Salt and fresh-milled black pepper

Heat oil in small saucepot over medium heat, add garlic, and sauté for 5 to 10 seconds. Add tomatoes, season with salt and pepper, add tomato juice, and bring to simmer for 5 minutes. Fold in scallions. Remove from heat, and keep warm, until ready to serve.

Chipotle Chili Polenta

Serves 6 • Preparation Time: 15 minutes • Cook Time: 40 minutes

3 tablespoons unsalted butter

½ cup small dice onions

4 cloves fresh garlic, minced

3 cups chicken broth

1 cup polenta

½ teaspoon chipotle purée

¼ cup grated Parmesan cheese

Salt and fresh-milled black pepper

Melt 1 tablespoon butter in medium saucepan over medium heat. Add onions, and sweat for 4 to 5 minutes. Add garlic, and cook for 1 minute. Add chicken broth, and bring to boil. Slowly stir in polenta. Return to simmer, and cook for 20 minutes, stirring occasionally. Season with salt and pepper.

Stir in chipotle purée and remaining butter into polenta, and fold in cheese. Keep warm, until ready to serve.

Asparagus

(See Fresh Asparagus recipe on page 345)

Baby Carrots

Serves 6 • Preparation Time: 15 minutes • Cook Time: 12 minutes

6 carrots with tops

6 cups water

1 tablespoon salt

2 teaspoons butter

Salt and fresh-milled black pepper

Trim all but ½ inch of greens from carrots. Peel carrots, and trim to 2 ½-inch lengths. Using a peeler, round off bottom cut of each carrot. Set aside.

In medium pot, bring water and salt to boil. Place carrots in water, and boil for 4 to 5 minutes, or until tender. Remove with slotted spoon, and place in bowl of ice water. Once cold, drain and cut carrots in half lengthwise.

Melt butter in a medium sauté pan over medium heat. Gently toss in carrots, season with salt and pepper, and sauté until heated through.

To Plate:

Place a scoop of polenta off-center on a warm dinner plate. Position asparagus and baby carrots on one side of the polenta. Ladle sauce on plate next to vegetables and polenta. Unwrap chicken, slice into 5 slices, and fan on top of sauce against polenta.

DINNER
in honor of
THE RIGHT HONORABLE
JEAN CHRÉTIEN, P.C., M.P.
PRIME MINISTER of CANADA

Maine Lobster
Applewood Smoked Bacon and Leeks
Lewis Cellars Chardonnay "Reserve" 1997

Pan Seared Bison Loin with Madeira Sauce
Wild Mushroom Flan
Crispy Potato Cake
Joseph Phelps "Insignia" 1994

Salad of Winter Greens
Avocado · Maytag Bleu Cheese · Sherry Dressing

Chocolate Hazelnut Terrine
Vanilla Sauce

THE WHITE HOUSE
Monday, February 5, 2001

Menu for dinner in honor of The Right Honorable
Jean Chrétien, P.C., M.P., Prime Minister of Canada.
February 5, 2001.

Pan-Seared Bison Loin with Madeira Sauce, Wild Mushroom Flan, Crispy Potato Cake, and Wilted Spinach

Wild Mushroom Flan

Serves 6 • Preparation Time: 30 minutes • Cook Time: 30 minutes

4 teaspoons unsalted butter, plus more for greasing

½ pound total shiitake, hen of the woods, and enoki mushrooms, cut into small pieces

2 teaspoons minced shallots

2 large eggs

1 egg yolk

1 cup heavy cream

½ teaspoon minced garlic

Hot water

1 tomato, peeled, seeded, and small dice (for garnish, optional)

12 chive tips (for garnish, optional)

Salt and fresh-milled black pepper

Preheat oven to 350°F. Grease 6 (2-ounce) soufflé cups or ramekins with butter, and set aside.

Melt butter in sauté pan over medium heat. Add mushrooms, and sauté for 2 minutes. Add shallots, and sauté for another 2 to 3 minutes. Remove from heat, season lightly with salt and pepper, and set aside to cool.

In medium bowl, whisk eggs and egg yolk together, add cream, continue to whisk, and add garlic. Season with salt and pepper.

Fill each soufflé cup ⅓ full with custard. Stir in 1 tablespoon of mushroom mixture into each soufflé cup. Fill soufflé cups with remaining custard.

Place the soufflé cups in 6 by 9-inch cake pan, and fill with enough hot water to cover ½ of the ramekins. Bake 30 to 40 minutes, until custard is firm to the touch. Remove from oven, cover, and let rest 20 minutes before removing custard from cups.

Crispy Potato Cake

Serves 6 • Preparation Time: 15 minutes • Cook Time: 15 minutes

Chef's Note: These potato cakes can be made 1 to 2 hours ahead of time and reheated in a 350°F oven for 4 to 5 minutes.

3 medium Idaho potatoes, peeled and reserved in water

½ cup unsalted clarified butter

Salt and fresh-milled black pepper

Preheat oven to 375°F.

Using a mandoline, julienne the potatoes. Place in medium bowl, and season with salt and pepper.

Divide butter into 2 (8-inch) oven-safe sauté pans over high heat. Add potatoes to pan, and pat down with the back of a spoon to ½-inch thickness. Cook 3 to 4 minutes per side, until golden brown. Place hot pan in oven, and cook for 3 minutes, then flip cakes, and cook for an additional 3 minutes. Remove cakes from pans, and place on cooling rack.

Madeira Sauce

Serves 6 • Preparation Time: 10 minutes • Cook Time: 15 minutes

2 teaspoons unsalted butter

2 shallots, thinly sliced

5 peppercorns

1 sprig fresh thyme

½ cup Madeira wine

1 cup prepared demi-glace

Salt and fresh-milled black pepper

Melt butter in medium saucepot over medium heat. Add shallots, and sauté 4 to 5 minutes, until lightly browned. Add peppercorns and thyme, and sauté another 2 minutes. Add wine, and bring to boil for 10 minutes, or until reduced by 80%. Add demi-glace, return to boil, and decrease heat to simmer for 5 minutes. Season with salt and pepper. Strain into another saucepot, cover, and keep warm over low heat.

Pan-Seared Bison Loin

Serves 6 • Preparation Time: 40 minutes • Cook Time: 15 minutes

3 (10-ounce) bison strip steaks

2 tablespoons canola oil

Salt and fresh-milled black pepper

Remove steaks from refrigerator 30 minutes before cooking. Season steaks with salt and pepper.

Heat oil in medium pan over medium-high heat. Place steaks in pan, and sear 4 to 5 minutes per side for medium rare. Transfer to plate, and rest for 5 minutes.

Wilted Spinach

Serves 6 • Preparation Time: 5 minutes • Cook Time: 5 minutes

1 teaspoon unsalted butter

1 pound of baby spinach, washed and dried

Salt and fresh-milled black pepper

Melt butter in medium sauté pan over medium heat. Add spinach, and season with salt and pepper. Stir until wilted.

To Plate:

Slice each steak into 10 slices, and fan 5 slices from center of plate. Invert flan on plate alongside meat, and top with diced tomatoes and chives. Cut potato cakes into 4 pie-shaped pieces, and arrange 2 pieces and wilted spinach next to meat. Top meat with mushrooms, and ladle sauce around meat.

Luncheon

Wild Mushroom Soup
Rock Shrimp
Basil Oil

Grilled Lamb Chops
Jalapeño Mint Sauce
Artichoke, Braised Endive and Baby Carrots
Potato Chive Purée

Mesclun Greens
Roasted Peppers, Olives and Feta Cheese
Shallot Dressing

"From Around the World"
Coconut and Chocolate Mousse Cake
Sweet Ripe Mango

Shafer Chardonnay "Red Shoulder" 2001

The White House
Tuesday, January 20, 2004

Menu for Television Correspondents Luncheon.
January 20, 2004.

Grilled Lamb Chops, Jalapeno Mint Sauce,
Artichokes, Braised Endive, Baby Carrots,
and Potato–Chive Purée

Jalapeno Mint Sauce

Serves 6 • Preparation Time: 10 minutes • Cook Time: 15 minutes

Chef's Note: This sauce can be prepared several days ahead of serving. I make my mint jelly from scratch, but due to the labor involved, you may wish to substitute a commercial mint jelly.

3 jalapeno peppers

1 (10-ounce) jar mint jelly

Grill peppers over open flame, until skin is charred on all sides. Place in small bowl, cover with plastic wrap, and let stand for 10 minutes.

Place jelly in small saucepan, and melt over low heat.

Scrape skin from peppers, cut pepper in half lengthwise, and remove seeds and stem. Small dice peppers, and stir into melted jelly. Pour jelly mixture into small serving bowl, and refrigerate until set.

Grilled Lamb Chops

Serves 6 • Preparation Time: 24 hours • Cook Time: 4 minutes

Chef's Note: It is best to marinate the lamb the day before to enhance the flavor of the meat.

4 sprigs fresh thyme

½ cup small dice carrots

½ cup small dice celery

1 tablespoon black peppercorns

4 bay leaves

3 (8-bone) racks of lamb, Frenched

2 tablespoons olive oil

Salt and fresh-milled black pepper

In a medium shallow dish, combine thyme, carrots, celery, peppercorns, and bay leaves. Cut lamb into 8 equally sized chops. Toss chops with herb mixture. Drizzle with olive oil, and mix well. Cover and refrigerate overnight.

Remove chops from refrigerator, and scrape off marinade. Heat grill to medium-high heat. Season chops with salt and pepper. Grill chops for 1 to 2 minutes per side. Remove from heat, and let rest for 10 minutes before serving.

Artichokes

(See Artichoke recipe on page 262)

Braised Endive

Serves 6 • Preparation Time: 10 minutes • Cook Time: 30 minutes

4 cups chicken broth

1 sprig thyme

2 bay leaves

1 teaspoon black peppercorns

3 endive heads

1 tablespoon unsalted butter

Salt and fresh-milled black pepper

Preheat oven to 350°F.

Bring chicken broth to boil in medium oven-safe saucepan. Add thyme, bay leaves, peppercorns, and a pinch of salt. Return to simmer, and add endive. Cover and place in oven for 15 minutes, or until tender. Remove from oven, uncover, and let cool. Remove endive from broth, gently squeeze out excess liquid, and set aside.

Melt butter in medium sauté pan over medium-high heat. Just as butter is about to brown, add endive, and brown on all sides. Season with salt and pepper. Split each endive head in half for serving.

Baby Carrots

(See Baby Carrots recipe on page 349)

Potato-Chive Purée

Serves 6 • Preparation Time: 15 minutes • Cook Time: 20 minutes

4 medium Yukon Gold potatoes, peeled and large dice

1 teaspoon salt

¼ cup heavy cream

3 tablespoons unsalted butter

¼ cup chopped fresh chives

Salt and ground white pepper

Place potatoes in medium pot, cover with water, and add salt. Bring to boil, reduce to simmer, and cook 10 to 15 minutes, until just tender. Drain potatoes, and set aside.

In small saucepot, heat cream over medium heat, until hot.

Using a food mill, purée potatoes into a medium pot. Add butter, and season with salt and pepper. Add cream, and stir thoroughly. Check consistency, and add a bit more cream, if potatoes are too stiff. Fold chives in, just before serving.

To Plate:

Spoon potato purée onto warm dinner plate at the 1 o'clock position. Arrange vegetables next to the purée. Place lamb chops against purée, crossing the bones.

Pistachio-Crusted Lamb Chops, Roasted Garlic Merlot Sauce, Braised Hearts of Celery, and Wild Mushrooms with Yukon Gold Potato & Celery Root Purée

Christmas Dinner

Nantucket Bay Scallops
Angel Hair Pasta
Saffron Mussel Sauce

PONZI CHARDONNAY "RESERVE" 1999

Pistachio Crusted Lamb Chop
Roasted Garlic Merlot Sauce
Braised Hearts of Celery
Wild Mushrooms

PRIDE MOUNTAIN CABERNET 1999

Salad of Endive and Watercress
Tart Cherries   Lemon Shallot Dressing

Hot Chocolate Soufflé
Raspberry Sauce   Whipped Cream

THE WHITE HOUSE
Friday, December 6, 2002

Christmas Dinner Menu. December 6, 2002.

Pistachio-Crusted Lamb Chops

Serves 6 • Preparation Time: 20 minutes • Cook Time: 60 minutes

¼ cup dry fine breadcrumbs

1 teaspoon minced fresh thyme

¼ cup pistachios, peeled and ground

1 tablespoon unsalted butter, melted

3 (8-bone) racks of lamb, Frenched, cap fat removed

2 tablespoons canola oil

2 tablespoons Dijon mustard

Salt and fresh-milled black pepper

Preheat oven to 375°F. Combine breadcrumbs, thyme, and pistachios in shallow bowl. Moisten with melted butter, and set aside.

Season racks with salt and pepper. Heat oil in large sauté pan over medium-high heat. Sear lamb on all sides, until nicely browned, 6 to 8 minutes total. Transfer lamb to small sheet pan, and place in oven for 15 minutes, or until meat thermometer reads 120°F. Remove from oven, and let rest for 5 minutes.

Liberally smear meat side of each rack with mustard. Roll each rack in breadcrumb mixture, and return to baking sheet. Return to oven, and bake for 5 to 10 minutes, until meat thermometer reads 135°F to 140°F. Remove from oven, and let rest for 15 minutes before serving.

Roasted Garlic Merlot Sauce

Serves 6 • Preparation Time: 15 minutes • Cook Time: 30 minutes

Roasted Garlic:

10 garlic cloves, skin on

2 teaspoons extra virgin olive oil

Preheat oven to 350°F.

Toss garlic and olive oil together in medium oven-safe sauté pan. Place in oven to roast, stirring every 2 minutes, until garlic is soft and golden brown (10 to 15 minutes). Remove from oven, and transfer to a plate to cool.

Once cooled, cut root end from cloves, and peel. Using fingers, press peeled garlic through a small fine mesh strainer into small bowl, and set aside.

Sauce:

2 teaspoons unsalted butter

2 shallots, peeled and thinly sliced

6 black peppercorns

1 sprig fresh thyme

½ cup merlot wine

½ cup prepared demi-glace

1 teaspoon cornstarch, dissolved in 1 tablespoon water

1 tablespoon puréed roasted garlic

Salt and fresh-milled black pepper

Melt 1 teaspoon butter in a small saucepan over medium heat. Add shallots, and sauté for 2 minutes. Add peppercorns and thyme, and sauté another 3 minutes. Add wine, and reduce by 75%. Add demi-glace, and simmer over medium-low heat for 5 minutes. Season with salt and pepper.

Gradually add cornstarch mixture, and return to boil over medium heat, stirring constantly, until sauce coats the back of a spoon. Remove from heat, and strain into another small saucepan.

Heat strained sauce over medium heat, and stir in roasted garlic and remaining butter. Remove from heat, cover, and keep warm, until ready to serve.

Braised Hearts of Celery

Serves 6 • Preparation Time: 10 minutes • Cook Time: 30 minutes

Chef's Note: Celery hearts are commonly available and are a popular vegetable in my hometown of Lancaster, Pennsylvania. I wanted to find a different way of enjoying them, other than eating them raw or using them in soup. I experimented using a French braising technique for endive that has turned out to be very popular and has become one of my signature vegetable preparations.

3 medium hearts of celery, root intact

4 cups chicken broth

1 sprig thyme

2 bay leaves

1 teaspoon black peppercorns

1 tablespoon unsalted butter

Salt and fresh-milled black pepper

Preheat oven to 350°F.

Diagonally trim the tops from celery hearts, leaving about 5 inches in length, including the root. Reserve trimmings for another use.

Bring broth to boil in medium oven-safe saucepan. Add thyme, bay leaves, peppercorns, and a pinch of salt. Return to simmer, and add celery. Cover and place in oven for 15 minutes, or until tender. Remove from oven, uncover, and let cool. Remove celery from broth, and gently squeeze out excess liquid.

Melt butter in medium sauté pan over medium-high heat. Just as butter is about to brown, add celery, and brown on all sides. Season with salt and pepper. Split each celery heart in half for serving.

Yukon Gold Potato & Celery Root Purée

Serves 6 • Preparation Time: 15 minutes • Cook Time: 45 minutes

Celery Root Purée:

1 large celery root, peeled and medium dice

2 teaspoons salt

Place celery root in medium pot, and cover with water to rinse. Drain and cover again with fresh water. Add salt, and bring to boil over medium-high heat. Decrease to simmer for 10 to 15 minutes, until knife tender. Drain in colander, and let steam evaporate for 2 to 3 minutes.

Using a food mill, purée celery root into a medium bowl. Transfer to food processor, and purée until very smooth. Transfer to small bowl, cover, set aside, and keep warm.

Potato Purée:

3 medium Yukon Gold potatoes, peeled and large dice, reserved in water

1 teaspoon salt

¼ cup heavy cream

2 tablespoons unsalted butter

Salt and ground white pepper

Drain potatoes, place in medium pot, cover with fresh water, and add salt. Bring to boil, decrease heat to simmer, and cook 10 to 15 minutes, until just tender. Drain potatoes, and set aside.

In medium saucepot, heat cream over medium heat, until hot.

Using a food mill, purée potatoes into a medium pot. Add butter, season with salt and pepper, add cream, and stir thoroughly. Fold in celery root purée, until well incorporated.

Wild Mushrooms

Serves 6 • Preparation Time: 5 minutes • Cook Time: 5 minutes

Chef's Note: Shiitake, Hen of the Woods, and Oyster mushrooms are fairly common and usually readily available; they make a great combination for this dish.

1 tablespoon unsalted butter

½ pound mushrooms (may be one variety or a combination), cut into small strips

1 medium shallot, minced

Salt and fresh-milled black pepper

Melt butter in medium sauté pan over medium-high heat. Add mushrooms, and sauté, until lightly browned. Add shallots, and sauté for 1 minute. Season with salt and pepper. Keep warm, until ready to serve.

To Plate:

Spoon a medium portion of potato and celery root purée off-center on warm dinner plate. Lean ½ of a celery heart in purée with interior exposed. Slice racks of lamb into chops. Fan 3 to 4 chops around the other side of the purée. Ladle sauce around base of chops. Place mushrooms over the meat.

Tenderloin of Beef, Cremini Mushroom Sauce, Chestnut Spaetzle, Glazed Root Vegetables, and Broccoli

DINNER

Blue Crab Gratin
Corn and Leeks
Landmark Chardonnay "Overlook" 2002

Tenderloin of Beef
Cremini Mushroom Sauce
Broccoli and Chestnut Spaetzle
Glazed Root Vegetables
Saintsbury Pinot Noir "Garnet" 2003

Watercress, Boston Greens and Endive Salad
Amish Farmhouse Cheese

Mocha Crème Cake
Orange Sherbet
Raspberry Sabayon

"Dolce" 1993

The White House
Monday, January 10, 2005

Dinner Menu, January 10, 2005.

Tenderloin of Beef

(See Roast Tenderloin of Angus Beef Recipe page 258)

Cremini Mushroom Sauce

Serves 6 • Preparation Time: 15 minutes • Cook Time: 30 minutes

1 tablespoon unsalted butter

½ pound cremini mushrooms, quartered

2 shallots, peeled and thinly sliced

6 black peppercorns

1 sprig fresh thyme

½ cup Cabernet Sauvignon wine

1 cup prepared demi-glace

1 teaspoon cornstarch, dissolved in 1 tablespoon water

Salt and fresh-milled black pepper

Melt 2 teaspoons butter in medium pan over medium-high heat. Add mushrooms, and sauté for 3 to 5 minutes. Remove from heat, season with salt and pepper, and set aside.

Melt 1 teaspoon butter in a small saucepan over medium heat. Add shallots, and sauté for 2 minutes. Add peppercorns and thyme, and sauté for 3 minutes. Add wine, and reduce by 75%. Add demi-glace, and simmer over medium-low heat for 5 minutes. Season with salt and pepper.

Gradually add cornstarch mixture, and return to boil over medium heat, stirring constantly, until the sauce coats the back of a spoon. Remove from heat, and strain into another small saucepan. Stir in mushrooms, and simmer for 2 minutes over medium heat. Remove from heat, cover, and keep warm, until ready to serve.

Chestnut Spaetzle

Serves 6 • Preparation Time: 10 minutes • Cook Time: 25 minutes

1 cup all-purpose flour

1 tablespoon plus 1 teaspoon salt

½ teaspoon ground pepper

¼ teaspoon ground nutmeg

2 large eggs

¼ cup milk

½ cup chopped chestnuts

3 tablespoons unsalted butter

Salt and fresh-milled black pepper

In a large bowl, combine flour, 1 teaspoon salt, pepper, and nutmeg. In separate mixing bowl, whisk the eggs and milk together. Make a well in the center of the dry ingredients, and pour in the egg-milk mixture. Add chestnuts, gradually blend in the flour from the sides, and combine well; the dough should be smooth and thick. Let the dough rest for 10 to 15 minutes.

Fill large pot with water, add remaining salt, bring to boil, and decrease heat to simmer. Place ½ of the dough in a large-holed colander, and hold over the simmering water. Push the dough through the holes with a rubber spatula. Cook for 3 to 4 minutes, or until the spaetzle floats to the surface, stirring gently to prevent sticking. Remove spaetzle from pot with a spider or slotted spoon to another colander, and rinse with cold water. Repeat with remaining dough.

Melt butter in a large skillet over medium heat. Just as butter begins to brown, add spaetzle, toss to coat, and cook for 1 to 2 minutes, until lightly browned. Season with salt and pepper.

RECIPE INDEX